FISHER, PAUL.

EDUCATION 2000

Other Books in This Series

Paul Fisher

Education 2000

Educational Change with Consent

CASSELL

Cassell Educational Limited
Villiers House
41/47 Strand
London WC2N 5JE

First published 1990

British Library Cataloguing in Publication Data
Fisher, Paul
    Education 2000: educational change with consent. —
(Issues in education).
    1. Great Britain. Education
    I. Title II. Series
    370.941

ISBN 0–304–32317–9 (hardback)
        0–304–32265–2 (paperback)

Phototypeset by Input Typesetting Ltd, London

Printed and bound in Great Britain by
Biddles Ltd, Guildford and King's Lynn

Contents

Acknowledgements

With thanks to all at Education 2000 in Letchworth and Ipswich who were so generous with their time. Special thanks to Richard Dix-Pincott; I wish the teachers at my school had been so patient. And thank you to Gillie Macdonald of *The Times Educational Supplement* for putting me in touch with Education 2000.

Foreword: The purpose of this series

The educational scene is changing rapidly. This change is being caused by a complexity of factors which includes a re-examination of present educational provision against a background of changing social and economic policies, the 1988 Education Reform Act, new forms of testing and assessment, a national curriculum, local management of schools with more participation by parents.

As the educational process is concerned with every aspect of our lives and our society both now and for the future, it is of vital importance that all teachers, teachers in training, administrators and educational policy-makers should be aware and informed on current issues in education.

This series of books is thus designed to inform on current issues, look at emerging ones, and to give an authoritative overview which will be of immense help to all those involved in the education process.

Philip Hills
Cambridge

1 Ideas

Something odd is going on in the schools of Letchworth Garden City. The schools' minister Angela Rumbold visited them in April 1987. A year later Kenneth Baker, during his tenure as Secretary of State for Education, followed her. Then, perhaps even closer to the centre of power, came Professor Brian Griffiths who is Director of the Policy Unit at 10 Downing Street and therefore one of Margaret Thatcher's chief advisers. Sir David Hancock, the Permanent Secretary at the Department of Education and Science has been to see what's happening as has Eric Bolton, the Senior Chief Inspector of Her Majesty's Inspectorate. The three members of an evaluation team largely funded by the Department of Education are constant visitors and they are writing a report due for publication in September 1990.

Every one of the six schools in this Hertfordshire town 40 miles north of London has been host to an inexhaustible supply of politicians, industrialists, financiers, educationalists and journalists. The Letchworth pupils hardly notice when yet another stranger enters their classrooms; they've become used to the attention and ignore the intrusions that have come from being part of a new project which has put them at the centre of attention. What everybody has been witnessing is Education 2000, a bold educational experiment intended as nothing less than a model for the entire British secondary system. The most straightforward explanation of E2K (as everybody in Letchworth now calls it) is that it uses charitable donations to buy extra staff to allow for retraining across a town's schools. Four comprehensives and two private boarding schools have shared the extra money in a scheme which concentrates on the educational aims they have in common. This unusual co-operation is spiced with ubiquitous, value-free computing which, at the very least, convinces everybody of the project's commitment to modernity and, of far greater significance, acts as a catalyst for a new approach to education. 'From teaching to learning' is one of the favoured phrases to explain what is going on.

Aside from the inordinate amount of top brass to have stepped into Letchworth classrooms, it is impossible to extract any single component which identifies E2K in Letchworth as unique. It is the sum of many parts and what is unique is the way they have been bundled together. True, there are other towns where state and maintained schools co-operate, as now routinely occurs in Letchworth. Yet there can be few places where teachers, from state and private sectors and across every subject discipline, regularly meet together to discuss their teaching; and few towns where the territorially minded factions of the National Union of Teachers, the National Association of Schoolmasters and Union of Women Teachers and the Assistant Masters and Mistresses Association have negotiated as a team. Letchworth is absolutely unique in the enthusiasm E2K has generated from a teaching force grown weary of educational initiatives. For here teachers have been encouraged to take school computers home with them and have been given the incentive of retraining themselves without any new legal framework compelling conformity with central government directives. Most Letchworth teachers approve of E2K, if only for the technology it has bought them, but there is room for dissent, for this project doesn't demand unanimity. It is too broad and too consensual to represent any one of the jargon-laden orthodoxies that threaten to crowd out teaching's soul.

Private capital increasingly plays a part in state education but nowhere else under a coherent directorate of a local firm (British Aerospace) with the sponsorship and participation of town worthies (Letchworth Garden City Corporation). Industrial donations have given Letchworth schools a greater density of computers to pupils than anywhere else in the country except for a handful of private schools and the City Technology Colleges. And there are no schools in any British town, aside from those in Letchworth, to have been linked together by a hefty minicomputer conferencing system. Admittedly it is being used as a sixth-form dating service as much as a distance learning network for, say, maths teachers. All these computers are the most visible part of the changes wrought by Education 2000, though teachers constantly stress that it is not merely a technology-driven project.

The technology of word processing played a part when E2K started with a conference at the University of London's Westfield College in the summer of 1983. The delegates split into study groups to produce word-processed papers which were then rushed into a book before the year's end. *Education 2000: A Consultative Document on Hypotheses for Education in AD 2000*[1] is a pot-pourri of a book where the text is as prolix as its title. But what it lacks in coherence it makes up in urgency. The conference, which was sponsored by the Duke of Edinburgh, eschewed 'taking up any party political stance'. It had to, for the delegates were well and truly divided by their politics. Industrialists and educationalists met on the understanding that while they wouldn't 'provide, between them, a single view' they would nonetheless try to discover points of agreement. What emerged was a consensus of disquiet with a genuflection toward the altar of new technology.

It is worth filleting the conference's book for the educational deficits which are identified, to show how little has changed in the intervening six years and how starkly and excitingly Letchworth differs from anywhere else in the country. The book pointed to the disgruntlement of the predominant group of pupils who leave school without having succeeded in any public exam. Many leave education unskilled for any employment and many are also leaving unfitted for life itself. The conference suggested that for the great majority of students the curriculum should have an 'intrinsic motivation' and a 'real and practical value'. At a time when unemployment was heading up to 4 million, they said this was especially true for those who may never get a job.

Success, as defined by access to higher education, is about 11 per cent in this country compared with nearer 30 per cent for the countries with which we compete. 'Why,' asked a paper whose compilers included IBM and Ford Motor Company executives plus teachers from the private and maintained sectors, 'should some 40 per cent of the school output be deprived of any meaningful measurement at all?' They further wondered why universities, which accept such a small minority of pupils, effectively determine the measurement apparatus for the rest. 'The immediate priority,' they concluded, 'is to make available to all throughout the country educational opportunities that are at present available only to some. This will require the switching of resources between and across educational sectors, though not necessarily total financial outlay.'[1] This was the sum of what the conference had to say about money to pay for the pragmatic idealism; the question of funds was to come later.

The conference turned its attention to teachers working in a system which encourages insularity and recommended that 'training and background should reflect wider life experiences than at present'. They anticipated the time when new technologies would supplement the work of schools and force a reappraisal of the differing roles teachers will play. That implies a greater depth of skills, which in turn means a greater investment in training.

The conference delegates also looked beyond schools. Industrialization, one group reported, had meant that from being the major employer agriculture now absorbs less than 3 per cent of the workforce. They looked to nineteenth-century educational values, suggesting that the primary purpose of education for an industrial society was to instil the characteristics of obedience, repetition and punctuality without which production lines would not have rolled. Whether that is true or not, they endorsed an apocalyptic view of the future asserting that survival, in both a national and a personal sense, would demand something different of schools. The post-industrial automation of manufacturing and clerking and the fragmentation of the old-style Mum, Dad and two-point-something children family has put us 'in a state of transition in which we are experiencing another major change in the framework of society. Unlike the developments of the industrial era, which had its traumas, the rate of change is very rapid and the time for adaptation is short.' Change, they felt, would become a way of life and something schools would have to prepare their pupils to be comfortable with. They had no great faith in the Government, which they saw as suffering from tunnel vision, where 'decisions are taken with a single objective in view [which] when put into effect conflict with a completely different objective being encouraged by another arm of government'. They demanded a broad view and a new scheme to co-ordinate the efforts of educational, training and industrial bodies. 'This,' they said, 'is urgently required to bring about the changes in the patterns and provisions of education which our developing society needs over the coming two or three decades. By AD 2000 anyone who wishes to work will need retraining at some time.'

Letchworth has provided an exemplar of some of these visions. Taken together its schools are the most technologized anywhere in the country and its children complement their computer literacy with an unusual openness. Almost all the Letchworth teachers have had some retraining and many have done work placements to gather experience of a world outside their institutions. This has involved local businesses, which in turn have visited the schools in unprecedented numbers at a series of breakfast meetings and on *ad hoc* classroom visits. With the staff retraining and invigoration and the regulated injection of computers and other technology, 'changes in the patterns and provisions of education' have been tested. If the Letchworth lessons, which are already being applied in Ipswich, are taken elsewhere, that Westfield conference in 1983 could prove of seminal importance.

Of course there is nothing new about the clamour at Westfield and its attendant analysis of how Britain lags behind its competitors. Nor is there anything new about blaming an inadequate education system for precipitating the nation's relative decline. Take for example this quotation from the French historian Elie Halévy:

> It was no longer possible to pass over the fact that a young Englishman on leaving school was intellectually two years behind a German of the same age with the consoling reflection that he made up in character what he lacked in information and that, if more ignorant, he was better equipped for practical life. How was it that in London itself the business houses of the City employed a host of Germans whose presence was unwelcome but whose industry compelled admiration? If English bankers and merchants preferred them to their fellow countrymen, it was because they found them less devoted to sport, more industrious, more methodical and better educated. England was beginning to lose confidence in herself. A nation of amateurs was being forced to recognise that they could not compete with a nation of professionals.[2]

The England Halévy was writing about, in 1912, was that of Queen Victoria.

A skim through the works of educational pundits reveals more of the same. A departmental committee in 1917 lamented Britain's 'educational and industrial chaos'. The Hadow Report in 1926 noted: 'School and industry are different facets of a single society, and the habit of mind that isolates them from each other is a habit to be overcome.'[3] The beefing continued through the Spens Report of 1938,[4] the Norwood Report of 1943[5] and the 1959 Crowther Committee which concluded that 'England cannot afford to be content with any aim lower than that of having, within 20 or so years from now, half its young people continuing in education until they are 18.'[6]

1979 came and went, that aim entirely forgotten. More recent context for the Westfield College conference was the Great Debate, initiated by James Callaghan in his prime ministerial Ruskin College speech in October 1976. He was both anticipating mounting criticism of secondary schooling and giving voice to concerns that education had got itself lost. By 1983 the Great Debate was being dominated by the then Education Secretary, Keith Joseph, who with his hesitant manner and combative ways was setting out to 'cut the fat' from what he saw as a flabby monster. An emphasis on standards and the possibility of schools opting out from their local authority became the politically advantageous order of the day. The Great Debate had gathered political intensity but still, as at Westfield, there was a continuum of vexation from the right to the left. Gone was any sense of celebration that for the first time in British history all children had the chance of formal education until young adulthood.

Increasing rancour crept into educational debates and the Westfield conference was all the more remarkable for hammering out an apolitical consensus of disgruntlement, formed as it was of disparate individuals from industry, commerce and education. They shared a concern that British education was in a blind alley and that the normal mechanisms for change were insufficient to allow it to break out. A bandwagon had started to roll. The late Sir Basil de Ferranti, chairman of Ferranti and the European member of parliament for Hampshire, became president of the Education 2000 trust. A clutch of vice-presidents included Lord Gregson, the chairman of the House of Commons Select Committee on Science and Technology, Hugh Metcalfe, a deputy chief executive of British Aerospace, and Neale Raine, who was Chairman of the Business and Technician Education Council. Education 2000 was registered as a charity dedicated to long-term planning for the country's educational needs in the twenty-first century and fund-raising began.

Others became involved. A fund-raising brochure prepared by Brian Dowling of the public relations department of the Kleinwort Benson merchant bank (this was during Big Bang and before Black Monday, insider dealing scandals and general suspicion of the City) restated British educational deficits more entertainingly than the Westfield book. 'There is neither point nor justice in seeking to apportion blame,' he wrote. 'The educational establishment and the teachers in our schools are not to blame.'[7] It was precisely the kind of thing teachers needed to hear at a time when an Education Reform Act was being framed and which the vast majority of them took as a government vote of no confidence in their devalued profession. 'Teachers work within a system which is rooted in academic achievement and access to our great universities, and which was established for a totally different society in centuries past,' said the man from the City.

> Ours is a society, moreover, which was never disturbed, as were those others with whom we collaborate and compete in the world, by violent revolution. They work within a system designed to train the few administrators of an Empire we no longer have. As for the many, present day education developed as a means of keeping them off the streets, when humane legislation barred children from the mines and factories.

Education 2000 was doing its best to sidestep what was fascinating the teaching unions and the media, to concentrate on the wider picture. Again large cultural and economic changes were sketched out, followed by this message:

> We must abolish failure. We have to promote achievement at all levels of capability. We have to promote confidence in the management of one's own learning and in the relevance of our learning to the patterns of life and work. This is what Education 2000 exists for: educating people for change.

That final rhetorical flourish became the E2K slogan. Its aims were also defined in the glossy brochure in the kind of cumbersome committee-inspired phrase which is sometimes necessary to maintaining a consensus. It is: 'Community activity as the stimulus: information technology as the means: curriculum development as the result: and the needs of young people as the end.' The progression has formed the scheme for this book.

John Abbott, the trust's first director, is the man who more than anybody else has given the rhetoric, slogans and mission statements concrete meaning. Until 1985 Mr Abbott was headmaster for eleven years at Alleyne's school in Stevenage, 5 miles south of Letchworth down the A1. Although he was not at the Westfield conference, he was at a meeting in February 1985 when the E2K trust met with the Letchworth Garden City Corporation, the Hertfordshire County Council (HCC) and the headteachers of the Letchworth comprehensive schools to propose a project. During the previous months he had been on a secondment where the HCC had asked him to carry out a feasibility study into curriculum requirements for the twenty-first century. The study sought to show how a range of curricular initiatives could be drawn together into a coherent programme. It suggested that in an information-rich society pervaded by the new technologies, the role of schools would have to change radically to reflect expanding learning opportunities outside institutionalized education. In a tone which had great appeal to those who became his new paymasters at Education 2000, Mr Abbott talked of

> winning for formal education that level of public sector investment appropriate to the task [and] to help society to realise that increasingly it would be necessary for the whole community to share a responsibility to create rich learning opportunities for young people.[8]

Mr Abbott's determination as persuader, explainer, educational computing enthusiast and fund-raiser are central to an account of E2K, for the Letchworth experiment wouldn't have happened as it has without him. That, of course, could be a drawback for it begs the question of how the E2K model would fare under a less dynamic leader. 'An enthusiastic philosopher; a frustrating man forever flying educational kites; he'll get you going though', says one of his ex-staff members. According to John Banham, the Director General of the Confederation of British Industry 'talking to him is rather like taking a drink from a fire hydrant'. This is true though he's corny and self-dramatizing enough to hand out copies of Rudyard Kipling's poem 'If', by way of inspiration:

9

> If you can keep your head when all about you
> Are losing theirs and blaming it on you;
> If you can trust yourself when all men doubt you,
> But make allowance for their doubting too;
> If you can wait and not be tired by waiting,
> Or being lied about. . .

Mr Abbott had become headmaster at Alleyne's in 1974 when it was being reorganized as a comprehensive. He began his teaching career, after a private school education and a degree from Trinity College Dublin, as a geography master at Manchester Grammar School and he recognized then that British education 'reflected a divided society and is one of the most potent agents in dividing it still further'. It brought him to the view that 'learning is a personal activity while teaching by definition is something done to you by someone else'.

All along Mr Abbott claims to have remained essentially an apolitical man. Ask him his political allegiance and he'll reply that he's voted for all (not both) major political parties. Nonetheless both Lord Joseph's hostile 'fat cutting' educational remedies and Lord Young's claim that the nation's training could be left to the Manpower Services Commission moved him sufficiently to write a couple of angry letters. These forced him to the attention of bigger fish than he'd been used to dealing with at County Hall in Hertford, and Lord Young (of whom Mrs Thatcher famously claimed, 'he brings me solutions while other people bring me problems') replied by return of post inviting him to the Commission's office in London.

The new chairman of the MSC, the only quango of its kind to have flourished under the Thatcher administration, had a billion-pound annual budget to 'ensure that unemployment among young people under 18 will become a thing of the past'. In John Abbott, Lord Young must have perceived one of his fabled solutions, for he made him an offer nobody could have refused. He invited Mr Abbott to take a sabbatical on condition that he travel anywhere in the world and then join him in an audience with the Education Secretary, Keith Joseph.

Mr Abbott, who had already visited American high schools during his time at Manchester Grammar and discovered 'an easy informality of staff/pupil relations', headed back west in October 1985. His first visit to Pittsburgh followed up an article he'd read in the *Times Educational Supplement*. He found a scheme for centralization where the Schenley High School had been set up as 'teaching hospital', a centre of excellence to which teachers were seconded for a term at a time. 'It was an artificial environment,' he recalls, 'and one which the teachers didn't like one bit.'

His next stop was at the Carnegie Foundation for the Advancement of Teaching based in Princeton, New Jersey. They directed their British visitor a few miles down the road to Princeton High School and what Mr Abbott discovered there he has untiringly described as his 'road to Damascus' conversion:

> In the two days I spent in that school . . . I was aware of a great deal of learning going on. There was much movement between classrooms and libraries, the pupils were working in groups but there seemed to be little of the nineteenth century model of the teacher as instructor. The pupils stood tall because they had been given the confidence to be responsible; the teachers, with a renewed sense of their professionalism, were dynamic. I was amazed and humbled. When you are in the business you know what you are looking for. Those young people were confident, in a non-aggressive fashion; they were alert, sensitive, inquisitive, enterprising and fun. Not just the bright few, for these attitudes ran throughout the entire school.[9]

It is exactly the sort of reaction the Letchworth schools now elicit and Mr Abbott wanted to find out how it had been done. The Princeton High principal, John Sekala, began with a gnomic statement. 'We believe,' he said, 'in functional literacy for everyone. The future belongs to those who have mastered the art of learning; it is the building up of that art which is the task of schools. To achieve that every pupil needs four essential skills. The skills to think, to communicate, to co-operate and to make decisions.'[9]

11

John Sekala drew Mr Abbott's attention to three factors, which helped form a blueprint for Education 2000 in Letchworth where it was applied to not one but six schools. First came community and 'an intensive dialogue involving parents, employers, voluntary organizations, academics and the school's staff.' As a result, said the American principal, the town felt that the school belonged to them. Second was a proliferation of computers, with one terminal to every six pupils.

> Every essay ever written, every report ever published is done on a word processor. We do this not to create fluent keyboard operators but to exploit the technology to support the learning process. Once the teacher has commented on it, often at length, it is given a mark, but not until the pupil feels that the draft is the best he can produce. The mark reflects not just the quality of the finished text but the improvement made on his original effort.[10]

Mr Abbott, who had tried in vain to get computing accepted like this at Alleyne's, was fascinated. The staff retraining to make this possible was the third and, felt Mr Abbott, the most critical part of the Princeton High equation.

He'd learnt of the school's staff development policy, which was more about carrots than sticks. Of an 81-strong staff the school never had more than 70 of them working the timetable. That gave nearly 15 per cent of the time for retraining, or roughly one term in nine away from direct classroom contact. A few teachers attended university courses but the bulk of them worked with staff on new teaching projects or spent time with local employers. The Princeton head told Mr Abbott: 'We couldn't conceive how to run this school without a continuous, locally devised teacher development programme. It is this which has given us our vitality.' This was dynamite and Mr Abbott recognized it as a way of bringing about change to which British teachers could hardly fail to respond. He'd discovered a detailed model which could perhaps answer the worries from both inside and outside education and which could be used to match the good intentions of the Education 2000 trust.

On Mr Abbott's return to England, he kept his appointments with David Young and Keith Joseph, who were duly impressed. By this time, in a happy coincidence of interests, his study into fresh curricula had helped earn the commitment of the E2K trust to funding the first pilot in Letchworth. Mr Abbott, with his track record as a practising head itching for educational progress and a man moreover who commanded the ears of those in high places, was the natural candidate to head the project and he took up his post as director of the trust in September 1985. He gave himself a target of five years before deciding whether to return to his old trade of headmastering.

Notes

1 *Education 2000: A Consultative Document on Hypotheses for Education in A.D. 2000* (1983). Cambridge: Cambridge University Press.
2 Halévy, Elie (1912), quoted on p. 43 of G.C. Allen's *The British Disease* (1979). London: Institute of Economic Affairs.
3 Hadow, Sir W. H. (1926) *Report of the Consultative Committee: The Education of the Adolescent.* London: HMSO.
4 Board of Education (1938) *Report of the Consultative Committee on Secondary Education with Special Reference to Grammar Schools and Technical High Schools* (Spens Report). London: HMSO.
5 Ministry of Education (1943) *The Norwood Report.*
6 Ministry of Education (1959) *15 to 18. Report of the Central Advisory Council for Education* (England) (Crowther Report). London: HMSO.
7 Dowling, Brian (1987) *Education 2000: Educating People for Change.* IOW: Education 2000 Marketing and Communications Group.
8 Abbott, John (1984) *Towards a Secondary Curriculum Appropriate for the Year 2000: A Summary of Main Points in the Feasibility Study known as 'Hertfordshire 2000'.*
9 Abbott, John (1988) 'The Cambridge Society: What should Cambridge be doing by the year 2000? Education as a life-long process.' Speech at Sidney Sussex College, Cambridge.
10 Abbott, John (1987) 'Industry/schools partnership for excellence.' Speech at the CBI National Conference.

2 Money and politics

After four years John Abbott had learnt a lot about the weary-ing business of fund-raising; soliciting funds had become a major preoccupation and he'd learnt that while all education initiatives are broke, some are more broke than others.

By 1989 results of the Letchworth experiment were there for many to see but, in a financial coitus interruptus, funds dried up. There was one computer to ten pupils, instead of the one to seven originally intended. More damagingly than this, the 1989 school year began with the enforced cessation of the Education 2000 training programme. As a mark of their reliance on Education 2000 techniques, the schools had rejigged their internal funding so that both private and state schools retained their information technology co-ordinators. But many of the teachers felt betrayed as they'd expected another two years' worth of their special training arrange-ments.

Elsewhere plans to transplant the Letchworth lessons to somewhere northern and urban like Bury or Calderdale or Leeds remained on the drawing-board. The one marker of progress lay down south in Ipswich where an original E2K sponsor, the Willis Faber insurance group, had helped convince the Suffolk County Council to go ahead with a project based on the one in Letchworth. The Ipswich people had to handle their own fund-raising separately from the trust for there was no way that the trust could justify spending charity money in another town even more prosperous than Letchworth.

While it hadn't considered fund-raising directly the Westfield conference had been correct in sensing a wellspring of commercial concern which was open for conversion into charitable cash. Education 2000 was always going to be a difficult notion to sell. State education is perennially unpopular, nowhere more so than among prospective donors usually wealthy enough to send their own children to private schools. Education 2000 also had to cope with an opposing suspicion from teachers that donations would come attached to a hidden agenda. John Abbott goes through an ideological minefield here and has cultivated a deliberate ambivalence about private sector funding.

On the one hand he travelled to venues like the Confederation of British Industry conference, where he berated delegates for allocating a meagre average of 0.2 per cent of their pre-tax profits to charity: 'American businesses,' he reminded them, 'donate ten times that amount.'[1] With such logic he has played a large part in wooing the likes of Woolworth, Allied Lyons, Glaxo, Prudential and W. H. Smith into giving five-and six-figure sums. Additionally Letchworth Garden City has given the project administrators free accommodation, and British Aerospace and the HCC have funded secondees. He can out-business-babble the best of them with talk of mission statements and enablement, and can charm business lunches with parables about the unpredictability of change, such as this:

> Let me tell you a story. Many years ago, in 1927, Mercedes Benz produced 1,700 cars. With amazing long-term vision the directors called for a report on the company's growth potential over the next fifty years. Eventually the report came back. By 1977, it said, technological change could make possible the production of 40,000 cars a year. The directors were appalled at the report which they saw as being naive. How could the schools ever train 40,000 chauffeurs a year, they wondered. We may smile at some of these assumptions, but are we sure that we can do any better?[1]

His punchline was that the twenty-first century is little more than a decade away. Altogether more than 100 different companies have been persuaded to make donations which have amounted to £1.49 million (see Appendix 1).

But the ambivalence remains. Push John Abbott and there's something close to a disclaimer of the whole grubby business of education rattling the begging bowl in corporate boardrooms. 'I do not believe in double finance,' he told me. 'Education 2000 is risk capital but you shouldn't expect industry to permanently bail out the state. But this sort of charitable seed funding is vital because government can only follow powerful ideas.'

For reasons we will consider later, the trust has only been able to raise 60 per cent of Letchworth's target budget though this should be recognized as a failure in fund-raising rather than a failure of the project itself; the seed money has undoubtedly germinated some powerful ideas. Once the trustees realized that £2.5 million was aiming too high, the first revised budget came out at nearly £2 million and was split, in 1985 prices, as follows:

1985–86	£200,000
1986–87	£800,000
1987–88	£800,000
1988–89	£50,000
1989–90	£50,000

This was to have provided 10 per cent extra staffing in the peak years and a total of 550 computers. Instead what happened is that the teachers' dispute intervened to delay the project's start by a year and the money never flowed as readily as had been hoped. The £1.49 million which was raised has been spent as follows:

1985–86	£80,000
1986–87	£350,000
1987–88	£580,000
1988–89	£480,000

A management committee meeting in November 1988 anticipated spending a further £970,000 by the end of 1992 but that seems unlikely. So, the cash listed in the second chart has bought 300 computers and had extra staff to cover time outside the classrooms which peaked at 7 per cent. To administer this extra activity Letchworth developed a 'fibrous management structure [which] seeks to use those techniques with teachers that it hopes they will use themselves with students' (see Appendix 2). A Central Project Management Team comprised the project manager and co-ordinators for the four components of the programme to handle the community, information technology, needs of young people and curriculum development (the first two as full-time posts, the second two half-time). Each school then appointed its own four co-ordinators, with that for information technology on a half-time basis and the others varying from half a day a week to two days a week. Two consultants – one for education and one for technology – were employed part time and the weekly meetings of the Central Project Management Team were mirrored (with less frequency) by meetings of the co-ordinators for each component with six colleagues from the other schools. It has all brought considerable privileges, both in extra time for the teachers and extra computers for the whole schools. However, some favourable number-crunching shows that Education 2000's privileges have not been outrageously expensive. That £1.5 million worth of private donations divides ino £420 per pupil spread over the project's four years. Or £105 per pupil per year, which is just over one-sixteenth of the Herts annual expenditure of £1,700 per pupil. If Education 2000 is indeed the powerful idea which a government should follow with central funding, the 6.25 per cent increase in expenditure is the sort of extra funding which it would have to consider.

In Ipswich, where the second Education 2000 model is being put into place, plans for slightly over £3 million expenditure have already been backed up by £750,000 of working capital. The Suffolk County Council has provided £250,000 of this money and looks likely to be more supportive of the second Education 2000 project than the Herts County Council has been of the first. By the end of the 1993 school year, the Ipswich budget will have split as follows: £285,900 will have been spent on administration costs including project director-

17

ate salaries, offices and marketing; £1.034 million will have been spent on computers and related technology; £179,000 on group, community and business placements; and, giving a clear indication of the priority placed on staff development, £1.6 million will have been spent on staff training. Staff first, then computers is one of the things Ipswich has taken from Letchworth, where £180,000 has been spent on equipment and £200,000 on additional staffing.

To persuade industry and commerce to pay for teacher retraining as well as computers is a difficult selling job. Unfortunately for Education 2000 it became doubly difficult when the government also discovered the powerful idea that industry might be persuaded to bail it out all over the place. The time when Education 2000 started looking for money coincided unhappily with a host of government-sponsored inner-city initiatives, many of them dependent on corporate generosity. Politicians such as Michael Heseltine repeatedly stressed the 'responsibility of private industry to respond to local demands', with the implicit message that healthy communities make healthy businesses. A nice message to hear at Rotary Club dinners but there came a point when industrialists turned on their own political party to point out that a major duty of governments in power is to organize welfare and education. The depth of the corporate pocket is not limitless, and appeals to those whose first professional duty is to make a profit can only go so far before straightforward business horse sense will rebel against being taxed twice over.

The private sector's understandable reluctance to fund education in a systematic long-term fashion is something the trust, as well as John Abbott, recognizes. In one statement from 1987 it said:

> The trust does not believe that it should be necessary, in the long run, for education to be dependent on the success, or otherwise, of raising supplementary monies from private sources. It does, however, see every reason why generous funds should be available to support powerful local initiatives within education which, as a result of short term programmes, could find more effective ways

of using statutory resources. The trust believes quite passionately that there is much local initiative in the country with real potential which is nearly always stifled at birth because there are insufficient resources available to support it.[2]

The subtext to this is that there was only £1.5 million when they had wanted £2.5 million. Aside from money worries there have been political difficulties too. While the E2K philosophy is to establish partnerships to include schools, local sponsors, national sponsors, the trust and local education authorities, it has never been part of its design for LEAS to finance the whole project. However, what started with a 'gentleman's agreement' which would have had the Herts LEA co-operating with E2K in Letchworth has ended less happily, for tucked into the most recent financial report from Letchworth is a phrase hinting at a nasty story. 'In practice,' it says, 'the non-involvement of Hertfordshire County Council in providing resources, and the difficulties the trustees encountered in fund raising have led to continuous modification of the plan.'

Initially the trustees offered to provide for all those activities and resources which would have been additional to those which the Herts County Council might have been expected to fund through its normal programmes. The trust was, and remains, anxious to show sponsors that their money buys additional things to that which would normally have been provided. So it has to be careful not to allow sponsorship to be seen as an alternative to any other funding. The diplomacy of this approach led to conflict with the LEA, particularly over training schemes. 'Our philosophy of integration and bonding,' says John Abbott, 'challenged a variety of other programmes, initiatives and projects. Planning resources together to meet coherently stated objectives was too much for an authority used to treating each programme as a separate entity.' An example of this was the way Herts insisted that Letchworth's Technical and Vocational Education Initiative in-service training was centralized into short courses dependent on supply teacher release.

The trustees were dismayed during early negotiations when the Hertfordshire LEA introduced a clause stating that:

> Education 2000 would be responsible for raising all the funds to cover these [training and technology] costs . . .and . . . there would be no additional financial commitment on the part of the county council, direct or indirect, during the project, but its possible later extension, more widely in the county could involve additional expenditure.

As time passed the difficulty of drawing other initiatives in Letchworth into a common framework caused increasing problems. According to Mr Abbott:

> While the support of individual officers for the project has been of great value, many sponsors have remained convinced that the project could have been far less expensive. . . . If the authority had been able to agree to a greater pooling of resources within the project (and many declined to support it at all), their support might easily have covered the remaining £900,000 still needed to complete the Hertfordshire project.[2]

Personalities and political changes have inevitably had an effect on the launch of the project. Key personnel at County Hall, who had originally given early encouragement to John Abbott, either retired or moved on and were replaced by others who sought to establish their own agendas. According to someone within Education 2000, who insists that her views remain unattributed, 'personal enmity and jealousy to John [Abbott] has played a considerable part behind the scenes in the local education authority's lukewarm response to Education 2000'. She puts this into a broader political context:

> Under both local and national political influences, the existing Hertfordshire model, which was intended to devolve power away from the centre to semi-autonomous geographical divisions, is being eroded. More power has been assumed by the centre because government legislation has increased the pressure for competition between areas and between individual schools. This has resulted in an environment which cannot tolerate individual initiatives that are not immediately replicable across the whole authority. Thus

20

we have the paradox of a government which claims to be in favour of enterprise and initiative and then legislates into existence a culture which stifles these very things.

According to the more measured words of Mr Abbott:

We started within the authority, passionately convinced that our strategy would help all its schools win public support. That we have been regarded as an extraneous group, a bolt-on, has been extremely disappointing but maybe, unconsciously, we have started to show the structures that could evolve once the traditional role of the LEA has been reduced.

He suggests that perhaps the administrative ideal is a consortium of schools accountable to its local community in units of pupils counted in tens rather than hundreds of thousands.

These arguments can be taken further: education authorities are inevitably centralist and will argue that they cannot support initiatives in one area which are not replicated in all others. Thus Letchworth has been unsupported with extra cash because the same thing is not happening in Watford. This seems fair enough as the HCC has continued to provide the majority of funding for the Letchworth state schools. However, many within Education 2000 complain of a centralist obduracy and cast the LEA as a reactionary force preventing rather than promoting change. It is with the future of local financial management in mind (as well as the sour local relationships of the recent past), that one of the Letchworth management team asks: 'Should the next stage of local management be the abolition of LEAs altogether and the formation of American style local school boards?' Evidently events have pushed some in the project on to more contentious ground; this is more combative and less consensual than anything considered at the beginning of the project.

The case for educational reorganization must remain open, but what is of interest is that the changes in approach fostered in Letchworth have reached down, perhaps inevitably, into educational administration. While E2K might complain of the 'continuous modification of plan', and blame it variously on

21

lack of funds and political turmoil, its operation has yielded lessons which the original aims could hardly have anticipated. The Central Project Management Team turned literary as well as political when it took some comfort from Machiavelli, and reproduced this quote from *The Prince* in its 1987 Annual Report: 'There is nothing more difficult to take in hand, more perilous to conduct, or more uncertain in its success, than to take the lead in the introduction of a new order of things.'

Notes

1 Abbott, John (1987) 'Industry/schools partnership for excellence.' Speech at the CBI National Conference.
2 *The Hertfordshire Project: The Programme* (1987). Education 2000 (statement).

3 Competition from City Technology Colleges

The politicization of fund-raising was always going to be bad news for a charitable trust which discovered itself facing government competition in attracting donors. Meanwhile the potential donors were discovering ever more refined and practised ways of saying 'No'. The body blow, from which Education 2000 has never recovered, were the City Technology Colleges. These were announced in Autumn 1986 by the then new Secretary of State for Education, Kenneth Baker, at the Conservative Party conference – the pre-election conference where ministers were going flat out to prove to the electorate that they had a fresh agenda.

There is an endless and eventually fruitless argument about raising educational standards. Those on the right are sure standards are declining and hark back to a distant half-remembered past. Those on the left will talk about 'a mismatch between needs and provision' and, if they are more imaginative, perhaps recall the RAF reading tests of 1939, which a far greater proportion of sixth-formers would pass now than succeeded then. And we still won the Battle of Britain. Decline or not, the astute Mr Baker knew he was safe in pinning the educational part of his political career to the mast of raising good old-fashioned standards. The best way, as he saw it, of doing this was to lash state schools to the national curriculum and further buck up the secondary schools with some competition. Thus one of his first major announcements was that he would establish 20 City Technology Colleges (CTCs), with capital costs met 'wholly or substantially' by business and industry and running costs by central government. Mr Baker hoped this partly state-funded independent sector would 'magnetize' other schools and act as a spur to excellence for the remainder of secondary education.

The Department of Education published a pamphlet, *A New Choice of Schools*,[1] within weeks of an Education 2000 fundraising brochure. In many respects the appeal of these two documents is identical. CTCs are also charities; they too stress a deeper involvement with community. Education 2000 schools, by dint of their extra funding and status as special experimental cases, also appeared 'a distinct category of provision within the education system'. Although the original government proposals didn't quite anticipate the extent to which City Technology Colleges would develop a cross-curricular use of technology, the DES pamphlet said: 'CTCs will where possible also be used to establish the value and effectiveness of equipping schools with information technology hardware and software on a scale more extensive than is normal in the maintained sector.' Technology was also the single most compelling part of the Education 2000 sales pitch. True, Education 2000 went further than the first CTC proposals in calling technology a 'central component of the project [which] can be used greatly to improve learning and enrich and extend current curriculum practice'. Hair-splitting as far as outsiders were concerned, but the overall effect of the CTCs is that they have not just leached out potential Education 2000 donors, they have stolen its thunder as well.

It was impossible, except for somebody on education's inside track, to detect how profoundly the two schemes diverged. For potential sponsors there seemed little to choose between them but for the full force of a wholehearted government imprimatur that the one had while the rival, as E2K became, just about had Department of Education approval. Yet differ they do and their similarities are superficial.

From inception to introduction in Letchworth, Education 2000 has proved as non-ideological as anything could possibly be in such politically polarized times. But working towards a consensus isn't how Kenneth Baker got where he is today and his City Technology Colleges are a first-rate example of applied ideology. His analysis of education is that it is too 'producer driven' and inhibited by teachers, the teaching unions, local authorities and professional educationalists. Education 2000 operates from a different premise and builds on what is already there, both in comprehensive and independent schools, rather than starting from scratch with a bunch of ideas rushed together to meet the deadline of a speech at a party political conference. 'Most teachers,' to quote John Abbott again, 'are idealistic and we want to empower them to grasp back that idealism.' That has meant the incentive of time away from classes to retrain rather than the deal offered to staff of the City Technology Colleges who, it must be said, applied to the three existing CTCs in great numbers. They are employed by governing bodies which are empowered to negotiate one-off take it or leave it deals on pay and conditions. The colleges are not answerable to local education authorities and Mr Baker's hope that 'local education authorities and the promoters of City Technology Colleges should work together for the benefit of the communities they will both serve' is barefaced dissemblance. The CTCs were a challenge to the status quo and designed to be divisive.

City Technology Colleges are resented by the local education authorities whose power they usurp and by the less well resourced schools they compete with. Lawrence Denholm, whose job title is the first deputy principal (college and community) of Djanogly City Technology College in Nottingham, put a 'case for the prosecution' in an article in *The Times Educational Supplement*:

> CTCs, we must believe, are expensive and unproven: concentrate resources unfairly on privileged individuals at the expense of the mass of pupils; are irrelevant to real needs; and lay false claims to innovations already under way but uncredited in state schools. Bribing teachers, they poach qualified staff from the maintained sector, leach out the leaven of able children and supportive parents. A gross misuse of public funds, they are not even an efficient way for industry to contribute to education. Under-resourced local

education authorities face rate capping if they try to remedy the situation: yet they must benefit all children, cater to the ineducable and delinquent and not just a select group of the able and the docile. Mr Jack Straw, the shadow education secretary, has it that CTCS are a 'party political irrelevance . . . Trojan horses to undermine the provision of comprehensive education'. But they are Mr Baker's pets so they will not be seen to fail.

I also wrote articles for *The Times Education Supplement* which took me to the three City Technology Colleges in existence at the time of writing. My visits were during their first terms: 1988 for Kingshurst in Solihull; 1989 for Djanogly in Nottingham and Macmillan in Middlesbrough, when their work had barely begun.

The day I was in Nottingham, where Mr Denholm insisted that the new institutions would have a beacon effect on the surrounding area, the local paper ran a story about one of the pupils who had been banned from her local-authority-funded Saturday morning music lessons. Mrs Thatcher had just attended the opening ceremony and had told the *Nottingham Evening Post* how 'appalled' she was by this. The local authority, in a quick response, wondered why a pupil of a City Technology College which had benefited from a £7.65 million government investment should need county school facilities especially when Nottinghamshire had to make do with a capital budget of £5.13 million for 513 schools. Understandable resentment, though it was a shame to pick on an 11-year-old to make the point, the more so as the Djanogly budget hadn't stretched to violins. It was a good enough story to make *The Sunday Times* headlines the following week.

With this kind of national spotlight and their position as a political crucible, it is hardly surprising that the new schools felt a little under siege and that their headteachers were having to master the dubious art of public relations. Valerie Bragg in Solihull was the least adept at this game and needed persistent prompting before she'd reveal that she'd had £650,000 to spend on brand new laboratories, computers and video studios. I was so pleased to have learned this that I did some simple arithmetic; for just £2.9 billion – a shade more than the cost of a Trident submarine – England and Wales' 4,455 secondary schools could be similarly well equipped.

Mrs Bragg has cast her school, or college rather, as a metaphor for corporate life. The crisp burgundy and grey uniforms, which made the place seem like a film set of a grammar school, matched the immaculate décor she said she'd chosen. Heads of department were introduced as 'area managers' and wore plastic identity tags on their lapels to prove it. Staff meetings had become management meetings and, carried away by it all, one area manager even spoke of 'learning parameters and procedures'. Their 'special project' for that term was determinedly commercial. Teams of children were formed to 'research, produce and market Kefir yoghurt'; the advertising and marketing team, for example, was briefed 'to produce sufficient product to allow a full scale market research test'. Sufficient product? Market research tests? For 11-year-olds?

Despite this alien language, there was a lot of good teaching going on and the children, who had been selected to give a comprehensive-style range of abilities, were well motivated. For example in an English lesson 20 or so children were reading from a play called *Class War*. They stood when I entered, then got on with the reading, which one of them captured on video. Before turning to talk to me their teacher had urged more realism in this portrayal of a class ganging up on an incompetent teacher. I'm afraid I don't remember what she told me as I concentrated on the children who, unprompted, had continued working.

At Djanogly in Nottingham (named after Harry Djanogly, to honour this local businessman's gift of £1 million) there was less technology, though still a considerable amount of kit dotted around open-plan areas in the ludicrously named 'Heritage and Enterprise Pavilion'. Instead of the Kingshurst pupil-to-computer ratio of 2:1, there were three computers to each child and by 1994, when it has its full complement of pupils, there will be a ratio of about 6:1. This was Letchworth's target before it settled on a ratio of ten pupils per computer.

The City Technology College computers were chosen in different ways and it is worth keeping the detail in mind when considering Letchworth's technology strategy; Education 2000 was simultaneously more draconian than the City Technology Colleges in the central insistence on specifying Research Machines whilst being more liberal in leaving it to the teachers to determine the precise ways they assembled their various networks.

At Kingshurst Mrs Bragg picked all the kit to give an initial computer muster of three Amstrads, eight BBCs, 35 Acorn Archimedes and a network of 35 IBM PS/2 micros to link all the classes together. Additionally the 20 staff each had one of Sir Clive Sinclair's z88 laptop computers. At Macmillan in Middlesbrough there is a z88 for each of the 195 first-years and they are encouraged to take them away after school to do their homework on. That 1:1 computer-to-pupil ratio will go when the next first-years join in September 1990. At Djanogly the genial head, Matt Andrews, threw the question of computer purchase open for debate, which had split the new institution into two camps. The teachers favoured Research Machines, which has provided all the computers in the Letchworth schools, both for its software and its educational track record. Opposed to them were administrative demands, backed by sponsors who had never heard of Research Machines, for kit that would immediately run on the Ethernet cabling which is as intrinsic to the new building as its roof. Thus they ended up with two separate networks: a Research Machines one confined to the information technology room and a college-wide Apricot network.

No such problems at Macmillan CTC in Middlesbrough, which has the most coherent technology policy of the three existing CTCs. Least surprising are the 25 stand-alone BBC micros, bought because they are what teachers and pupils are most familiar with. According to Pat Cummins, the deputy headteacher responsible for Macmillan's computer strategy, 'it is a mistake to leap straight into the unknown'. She's made an educational leap though, for what makes Macmillan unique in secondary education is its broadband network which is designed to carry data and video channels simultaneously. The new building has 530 plugholes (or what they call 'information points') which hook up some 280 Amstrads, 53 television sets and eight video cameras. 'We chose broadband,' explains Mrs Cummins, an English teacher whose previous post was an information technology advisory one in North Yorkshire, 'because it allows all information to flow from the same source. This demonstrates the principle that information is essentially the same whatever the medium.'

During the first term Mrs Cummins' information technology scheme had pupils learning word processing easily on BBCs, Amstrads or their Z88s. The Amstrads were being used for word processing, electronic mail, administration work and games, and there was no intention of running educational packages until the second term. To prove that Education 2000 is not the only scheme to change some of its plans in midstream, this is not quite the way things were originally outlined. By the time Mrs Cummins was interviewed in January 1989, building work was well advanced on a pair of Department of Education specified information technology rooms. Mrs Cummins made an ultimatum: she insisted that she wouldn't join unless the IT rooms went because she was determined not to get involved with a new project which had information technology as a discrete subject. This has put her at the centre of a more severe battle, for the Department of Education grew cost-conscious when it learnt that broadband doesn't come cheap. Of the £250,000 Mrs Cummins spent on computer and associated technology, £130,000 went on the broadband cabling, a pair of Intel file servers and the circuitry to convert the Amstrad computers into machines that could use the same cables as televisions. Macmillan argued that the £130,000 should be included in building costs; the Department of Education procrastinates and the eventual computer-to-pupil ratio hangs on its decision for, unless that network infra-

29

structure is defined as part of the building, there will be no more money to buy computers when the next first-years start in 1990.

The DES wanted bold experiments and that is what Mrs Cummins is delivering. Of all the CTC teachers I spoke to, she was the most keen to discuss the broader educational and political issues. Much of what she has to say echoes what is being said within Education 2000. For example, she favours the maximum access to technology which broadband should give because 'by not limiting teachers to applications which merely imitate teaching methods, they will be able to move away from the routine of performing teaching and begin the process of managing learning'. She justifies breaking away from teaching's mainstream by voicing her irritation with the same type of local education authority hierarchies that have frustrated Education 2000 in Letchworth. She condemns LEAS for being too ossified to make the big changes. 'We might have blown formal education in this country,' she says. 'City Technology Colleges could represent one last chance.' If this is the case, it will be a lot more expensive to share it round than Education 2000.

Casting aside the sense of embattlement in the new buildings, it is undeniable that the first three City Technology Colleges are impressive places. The new technology and the new enthusiasm were good to witness and I attempted to balance my overall scepticism about the schools' contentious constitutions with what I had seen in the classrooms. Maggie King, the headteacher of Stourport-on-Severn school in Worcestershire, wrote to *The Times Educational Supplement* of 20 January 1980 to say that she wasn't at all impressed by what I had reported on at Kingshurst:

A staff member was quoted as saying that nobody, staff or pupils, was 'switched off'. As anyone who has been involved at the start of a new venture is aware, success in the first year is almost a foregone conclusion. Staff are all newly promoted into their appointments, and the adrenalin flows readily in the first flush of enthusiasm. The new intake have been 'selected', and are flattered at being part of a fresh initiative, and there are no older pupils for whom the newness might have worn off. The success of a new idea is never proved during this first honeymoon period. For a school we must wait for the third or fourth cohort to progress through, which in the case of Kingshurst will be 1995 or 1996. By then, of course, Mrs Bragg will have long since left to join the Department of Education and Science, European Commission, or to become an MP.[2]

The jury is out both on the educational success of the new City Technology Colleges and on the future of Mrs Bragg's career, though she has continued to raise hackles with her proposals to enter her pupils for the international baccalaureate examinations. However, there is already a verdict on Kenneth Baker's promises to persuade private companies to pay 'wholly or substantially' for 20 City Technology Colleges. The verdict is one of failure, and an expensive failure at that. Industry just hasn't responded with the generosity Mr Baker banked on. John Harvey-Jones, when he was chief executive of ICI, was the most openly dismissive of City Technology Colleges and he spoke for many when condemning them as an inefficient way for industry to invest in education. Indeed, to echo Djanogly's first deputy principal (college and community), the funding of the City Technology Colleges has made them into 'Mr Baker's pets'. The Treasury is having to meet 80 per cent of capital costs to give a total bill in excess of £100 million. The CTCs established or in the pipeline are: Kingshurst, 1988; Djanogly, 1989; Macmillan in Middlesbrough, 1989; Tyneside, 1990; Bradford, 1990; Croydon (Selhurst Performing Arts), 1990; Sylvan (Harris Trust Croydon), 1990; Dartford, 1990; Glasgow, 1990; Swindon, 1990; Wolfson (site to be announced), 1990; Telford, 1991; Bacons (Southwark, London), 1991; and Haberdashers' Aske's (Lewisham, London), 1991. And this at a time when falling rolls are creating thousands of empty places in schools. It is small wonder that most teachers are hostile towards the mollycoddled City Technology Colleges, particularly at a time when they are struggling to come to terms with the national curriculum from which the CTCs as 'independent' schools are exempted.

Those within Education 2000 are jealously dismissive of the City Technology Colleges. Laurie Robinson, an Ipswich headteacher who did a year's secondment as project director of Suffolk 2000, says: 'Education 2000 gets all the advantages of City Technology Colleges without any of the drawbacks.' Richard Dix-Pincott, a former headteacher who moved on to become the associate director in Letchworth, says: 'With less money, we could have achieved across Nottingham what Djanogly is achieving in a single institution.' Put another way, the £100 million which is being sunk into fourteen City Technology Colleges could have set up 50 towns such as Letchworth where £1.5 million has had such an impact on six secondary schools, 250 teachers and 3,500 pupils. With the CTC money, some 300 schools could have been freshly stocked with technology and a re-enthused staff for, in terms of crude arithmetic, Education 2000 represents a twenty-fold increase in efficiency over the politicized City Technology Colleges.

Notes

1 *A New Choice of Schools* (1986). London: DES.
2 *Times Educational Supplement*, 20 January 1989.

4 Letchworth
'Community activity as the stimulus'

Community is one of the more slippery words to be used by social reformers. It is a catch-all used by anyone from proponents of the European Community to the local business community to try and persuade *us* that *we* have something, beyond living in a big and hostile world, in common. It is perhaps why the term community hardly got a mention in the 1988 Education Reform Act, yet formalized community activity – the attempt to pull in the parts of a town which other schools don't reach – is central to Education 2000. Its importance was made clear at the Westfield conference. 'The role of the community is vital,' the delegates agreed. 'The community must be fully involved; provide leadership, ideas and finance; provide security and effect the development of relationships. Industry and commerce must participate in the secret garden of the curriculum and thus sow the seeds of communal harmony.'[1]

In selecting Letchworth for its first pilot, the trust picked an unusually harmonious place. Letchworth is the middle of middle England but a town which, more than most other towns, can carry the label of being a community. It is insular and comfy but never quite boring and symmetrical. Its tree-lined streets, high-specification early century brick and wood architecture and its many public spaces reveal a legacy of liberal-minded philanthropic planning. A rational sort of place, therefore, to choose for Education 2000's late-twentieth-century version of consensual social engineering. Letchworth is a town built on a book. *Tomorrow: A Peaceful Path to Reform*, written in 1898, was reissued in 1902 under the less

boosterish title of *Garden Cities of Tomorrow*.[2] Its author,
Ebenezer Howard, was a parliamentary reporter who had
made a study of purpose-built industrial communities such as
Robert Owen's New Lanark, Titus Salt's Saltaire, Lever's Port
Sunlight and Cadbury's Bournville. John Abbott may not have
known it, but in his reliance on American models he was
following in Howard's footsteps: in the 1870s Letchworth's
founding father had travelled to America to study the rebuild-
ing of Chicago after a fire in 1871.

The rationale of Howard's book was that new towns should
be planned as 'garden cities' where thousands of trees were to
be planted as arteries through which the 'lifeblood of the
countryside could flow'. Populations, surrounded by an inviol-
able green belt, should be limited to 32,000; today Letchworth's population is 35,000. This was long before town planning became a devalued trade (in fact the Letchworth chief
architects Barry Parker and Raymond Unwin were founder
members of the Town Planners' Association) and Howard
schematized his idealism in diagrams specifying the balance
between rural and urban, patterns of employment and transport arrangements (see Appendix 3). He also made detailed
financial plans to ensure the development of his ideas with a
basic requirement that, in a phrase redolent of Education 2000
beliefs, the site belonged to the 'corporate community' where
any income should be returned to the corporate kitty.

In those days there must have been less red tape, for things
moved fast – a good deal faster than Education 2000. By 1905
Letchworth, which had formerly been three tiny villages, was
alive and the First Garden City Ltd 'Cheap Cottages' exhi-
bition showed off 114 dwellings to over 60,000 visitors. Building continued over the next three decades and Letchworth was
praised, or derided, much as Milton Keynes is today. Howard's
'master plan' envisaged a square of civic and religious buildings
to form a visual climax but by the time he died in 1928, First
Garden City was penny-pinching and so, like Education 2000,
some of the original targets were not reached. However, the
spirit embodied in his writing and diagrams, where he'd

imagined 'three magnets', remains. The first of these magnets was the town, the second the country and third, to blend the best elements of each, the town country. Like Education 2000, Ebenezer Howard felt that the fragments which make up society could be pulled together into a more coherent community.

Ebenezer Howard's magnet metaphor has, coincidentally, gained educational currency though it is not something Education 2000 approves of. A magnet school is given special privileges which are meant to attract better practice in the surrounding schools though many would argue they simply establish divisive competition. The City Technology Colleges are the best-known examples of recent educational magnets. Beacons or lighthouses, therefore, are E2K's favoured metaphors and that is why any E2K project must include all schools in an area. Semantic, maybe, but the magnet 'follow us' exemplar established by the town fathers made Letchworth an ideal place for the similarly broad-minded beacon-style 'follow us' philosophy of Education 2000. It is why, immediately after Letchworth agreed to host the first Education 2000 project, the town's two independent secondary schools were invited to participate. They joined in because nobody would want to reject a kindly gift horse bearing promises of training and brand new computers but they took a risk in becoming involved. They stood to lose if local parents interpreted their participation as meaning they would no longer offer something different from the maintained schools.

The Letchworth schools will be described briefly here, and in alphabetical order, to follow the Education 2000 example of not discriminating between public and state institutions. They are: Fearnhill; Highfield; Norton; St Christopher; St Francis; and Willian.

Fearnhill School, once described by a school inspector as a 'golf course school', is on the edge of town overlooking Howard's green belt. It is the ex-grammar school, has 700 pupils and the youngest staff of the schools, with a recent average of five maternity leaves per year. It has a long tradition

35

of progressive liberal education befitting its Garden City origins.

The Highfield School is a purpose-built comprehensive. When Peter Jackson became its first headteacher in 1965 he was, at the age of 34, one of the youngest heads in the country and his school is the most popular among Letchworth parents and children. With its good examination results and early commitment to technology and special needs education, it would have stood out as a model school even without the injection of Education 2000 money and ideals.

Norton School is the solid traditional ex-secondary modern which has a well established teaching staff few of whom are under 30 years old. Very much the local school drawing its pupils from the immediate surroundings, it has always had strong community links. Its notice-boards bristle with announcements of ballroom dances, sports events and family outings. Dating from 1909, it is the only remaining original Garden City school and it must be one of the only schools anywhere to have a thriving grandparents' association.

St Christopher has long put consensus, albeit a fee-paying version, into action. Founded by the Theosophical Education trust in the late 1920s, its educational aims are that 'members of different faiths shall be encouraged to mix together and in this way to learn a respect and tolerance for beliefs other than their own'. It is altogether a remarkable place. Its pupils are aged between 2 and 18; its vegetarian food has earned it mention in Egon Ronay's food guides; it employs an educational psychologist and has a long tradition of taking disadvantaged children who are in local authority care and whose home circumstances are so bad that boarding education is seen as of value. St Christopher, according to other teachers in the town, is playing down its image of trendy individualism to place greater emphasis on the academic. It is still trendy though, and among its pupils are sons and daughters of Monty Python actors and of Pink Floyd, the rock group which made so much money for its fatuous pop song 'The Wall' which began 'We don't need no education. . .'.

St Francis College was a Roman Catholic girls' boarding school and remains the only single-sex school in Letchworth. Founded in 1933 by Belgian nuns, it hit a crisis in 1983 when the nuns withdrew. It was reconstituted as a lay Christian school, though still preserving much of its Catholic ethos. However, in what may be another demonstration of Letchworth's traditions of tolerance, its present headteacher, Janise Frith, is not a Catholic.

Willian, the final school, is in its final crisis. It serves the Jackmans estate, most of whose residents moved there from slums in London's Tower Hamlets during the 1960s. This 'overspill' population has stayed put and grown old and, after a debate which has continued since the Hertfordshire County Council started its secondary review in 1984, Willian is the school most at risk from falling rolls.

Those within the project acknowledge that Letchworth is a rather peculiar town but assert that its representatively mixed range of schools has served as a normal enough bedrock to give their experiment status as a model for other, wholly dissimilar, towns. A comment made by those sceptical of Education 2000's self-appointed role as a beacon for the secondary sector is that it has been tested out within the comfortable confines of Letchworth. Yet the town's recent economic history is not that comfortable and the recession of the early 1980s dragged it closer to national norms with the closure of Borg Warner's factory and with it several other manufacturers. In their place the Enterprise 2000 business park was founded to attract light industry. And educationally it hasn't felt that comfortable either. Richard Dix-Pincott, who was acting head at Fearnhill until he became the project's associate director in April 1989, says: 'One of the major successes of the Education 2000 model is how it gives schools the resource and confidence to transcend major problems. I think it would be of value to highlight that what we have done has taken place in a very harsh climate.' He cites industrial action in 1985, the introduction of GCSEs, the 1988 Education Reform Act and 'almost the worst example of how to manage an LEA secondary review with three out of the four state schools being threatened in turn with closure'.

The secondary review could have split a town where the schools were less cohesive. According to one local industrialist quoted in a recent Education 2000 report: 'We don't want one school to opt out and become a prestige institution.' He argued with a self-interest enlightened by a direct application of Education 2000's ideals of community power:

> Children going to an opted-out school would most likely go off to further education and be lost to the town. The other three schools [Letchworth's two private schools are of course unaffected by the secondary review] might become sink schools. We couldn't tolerate that as they would be the source of our future employees. We want all our schools to be good and we want to help all of them, not just one of them.

There is a final peculiarity about Letchworth: the town constitution is unique in being protected by a special Act of Parliament. During the 1950s, when property values started to rise, First Garden City Ltd became vulnerable to property speculators and Ebenezer Howard's ideals of self-ownership and imaginative community development were in danger of being bought out by big business. The battle to save the town's integrity resulted in the formation, in 1962, of the Letchworth Garden City Corporation and assured the new managing body a predictable financial surplus. That corporatist philosophy underpinned by financial leeway also made it predictable that the chairman of the Corporation, Sidney Melman, should have responded to advances from the Education 2000 trust in 1984. The Westfield conference ideal of community involvement to 'provide security and effect the development of relationships' began to become a reality. From August 1985 the Garden City Corporation gave office space in its mahogany-panelled, neo-Georgian headquarters opposite the railway station, for administration of the Letchworth experiment. The following November, in another link-up of education and the broader local community, British Aerospace seconded one of its own employees, Jeanette Morgan, as project manager. When she left in January 1988 the notion evolved of a dual directorship with a project director from business/industry and an associate director from education. It was early demonstration of Education 2000's fluid hierarchy and 'fibrous management structure'.

Tom Corkill, a British Aerospace employee of 40 years' standing, was appointed project director, a post British Aerospace has continued to fund right up to the present. He trained as an engineer and in his time at British Aerospace worked on aerodynamics, project management, quality engineering, engineering management and finally as head of corporate education and training. He is a great believer in the virtues of co-operation and pulling together and he now spends a considerable part of his time organizing the many visits to the schools. He's seen a thousand people rubbernecking their way through Letchworth classrooms full of pupils busy at their computers and has grown used to the inevitable reaction that 'it wasn't like this in my day. I had no idea schools were like this.' He more or less has a script to inform his guests' amazement.

'The six schools,' he'll say to his educational day trippers, 'all lie within one mile of the town centre, so it is possible to call on three or four of them in the day to compare them with each other, what they are doing and, of course, relating school practice to the briefing message just heard.' As Mr Corkill stresses:

> Each school is unique. It is characteristic of the project that they collaborate and share skills and knowledge and the support provided by Education 2000 whilst undertaking the delivery of the curriculum in their own way. It is no part of the Education 2000 ethos to specify what should be taught or even to specify what should be done with the resources provided. The individuality and freedom of the schools is inviolate and it is believed that the schools' success in working towards the Education 2000 aims and objectives is due, substantially, to this autonomy.

Having established this point he goes on to explain the pres-

39

ence of the computers, where pupils 'learn by practice that information technology is destroying mental and physical boundaries. They can abandon the dryness of relying only on textbooks.' Mr Corkill talks of schools working together on curriculum development and invites guests to talk to the teachers and 'witness the bridging across the schools with the experience that each individual can offer to others. This collaboration has undoubtedly accelerated the pace and quality in the development of the curriculum, bringing to bear the resources that are needed.' By way of further example he plugs his own company and the placements it has organized, in conjunction with craft design and technology teachers, to 'share its own endeavours in the related fields of design, environmental testing and technical publications'.

Aside from the administrative commitment of British Aerospace and the Letchworth Garden City Corporation, there are many other examples of town and gown coming together under the Education 2000 banner. 'With the fast approaching end of the school year,' says an item in the North Herts Council for Voluntary Services' quarterly bulletin, 'it seems appropriate to thank the young people who give up their free time to produce this newsletter.' Thanks went to pupils from St Francis College, Norton School and St Christopher School.

There are several remarkable things behind this little notice. That pupils should partly write, illustrate and produce a newsletter for local charities is probably not unprecedented but that pupils from three separate schools should work together on such a project is remarkable. All the more so because two of the schools in the list are private and one, Norton School, is maintained. Prior to Education 2000 these schools had had no formal contact, except on the sports fields. Tom Szirtes makes his job as operator of the desk-top publishing computing package sound straightforward:

Each newsletter takes me seven or eight hours to put together on the computer. Some of the St Francis girls write the articles and the rest are tightening up copy the Council for Voluntary Services provides for them. Then they type articles so I can put them into my files. We've had one or two meetings in the Garden City office but I don't think I've met all the others who have been working on it.

He said he had advertised for more volunteers through the Ebenezer minicomputer network which has terminals in all six schools. Then he complained about the cluttered layout of the bulletin which he thought would have been greatly improved if he had worked to a tighter format. 'The community co-ordinator disagrees,' he says. So blame for typographical confusion, which I too think fell prey to overusing the bells and whistles of the Aldus Pagemaker software, belongs to Peter Cook.

Mr Cook is deputy head of Fearnhill School and from January 1987 to July 1989 was on secondment as Education 2000's community co-ordinator. His job was to breathe life into that first clause of the mission statement which prescribed 'community activity' as the first condition for change. His view is that

> Historically, the majority of adults have taken the view that teachers, even if they are not very popular, are the professionals in education and that they should therefore be left alone to get on with the business of educating children. Some parents have taken an interest in the progress of their own child and, of course, that interest intensifies if things go wrong.

Isolated events such as school reports, the occasional open day and formal parents' evenings normally serve to reinforce the separation of education from life outside the school.

A key exercise in the planning of the project was 'mapping the community'. From 1985 a group of six deputy heads, led (supported is the word many at Education 2000 would prefer) by the head of Highfield, Peter Jackson, met regularly to discuss the nature of the Letchworth community and to identify individuals and interest groups representing different opinions about the community's expectations of education and its young people. Their aim was to 'build a comprehensive community

41

dialogue to establish a consensus of opinion on the objectives for education and to provide for this broadly within an educative community'. That is, they were offering 'the community' access to what the Westfield conference had called the 'secret garden of the curriculum'.

Peter Cook had the tricky job of helping put this into practice and in September 1987 each school appointed two co-ordinators (each released from a tenth of their timetable commitments), to look after the 'school community' and 'industrial connections'. Mr Cook's was a nebulous task, but he reports some success. 'We have,' he claims, 'stimulated a far greater involvement and given the whole town an opportunity to discover what goes on in their schools.' First teachers and pupils met representatives of such bodies as the local Council of Churches, the Rotary Club and the police. The best-attended meetings were with local churches which produced a 'statement of faith'. Next came the links with local businesses though, says Mr Cook, 'against the backdrop of our wider community involvement, we tried to make this more than just another industry/education liaison scheme'. The links came in several forms. A series of breakfast meetings was inaugurated, initially in various locations, such as factory canteens, and then rotated through the schools. Just about everybody who is anybody in Letchworth has attended one of these and Mr Cook can produce pages and pages of those who, often for the first time since they finished their own education, stepped back through school gates.

The 1983 conference at Westfield thought that teachers needed 'training and background [to] reflect wider experiences than at present' and extended visits to local business and commerce had been part of that Princeton High School mix which so impressed John Abbott. Perhaps the biggest part of Mr Cook's job has been organizing one- or two-week placements for 50 teachers with the Education 2000 trust paying for supply cover while they were away. By and large the teachers decided where to visit. Mr Cook feels that it is both a reflection of the teachers' prejudices and of Letchworth's

economic life that few placements were in factories. The range
of places visited, however, was varied.

Peter Cook himself spent six days with Tesco. For the first
half of his assignment he was on a management training course
and then he went to work in a supermarket in Baldock. 'Yes,
I enjoyed it,' he says. 'I was able to gain an appreciation of
the general tasks involved in running a large supermarket.' He
says the course convinced him that the worlds of school and
retailing have as many differences as similarities:

> My impression was that the aim of the retailing organisation is
> relatively easy to identify and company policy gave a coherence to
> the operation. Education is not nearly so susceptible to ready
> definition of aims and objectives, and since so much depends on
> human personality and interaction within an institution, a greater
> variety of needs and approaches is found.

Hardly earth-shattering, but Mr Cook is a cautious man and,
as he had temporarily left the day-to-day school activities for
the more bureaucratic role of community co-ordinator, he
found the organizational aspects immediately useful. Other
teachers took back some experience they could use in the
classroom.

Anne Clarey, who teaches home economics at Highfield,
spent a week in the Food Hall at Harrods. The first day saw
her 'with a lot to take in' on a staff induction course and at
the end of the afternoon she found herself packing Harrods'
hampers. 'The pace was tough,' she reported after a day in
the restaurant when they had taken £2,000 by 3 p.m. 'Overall
a marvellous opportunity was created for me to see Europe's
largest store in action. I found the staff at all levels to be
friendly, helpful, patient and interested.'

Sue Plummer, a mathematics teacher at Highfield School,
spent four days on a local farm. She related what she saw
there straight back to the curriculum saying that links between
the farm and the school could help in several ways. For geography GCSE and A-level students she felt the farmer had much
to say about political and market issues; and for environmental

43

studies the farmer had much to say about conservation policies and the use of fertilizers. When she returned she worked with Thomas Thurman, a third-year pupil, on a farming simulation game to run on the school's computer.

Simon Studd, who taught chemistry at Norton School, spent five Fridays on visits to the Johnson Matthey chemical firm in Royston. Peter Cook asked every teacher who had been on an industrial visit to write a report and Mr Studd concluded his by saying:

> I was impressed (and surprised) at the emphasis on communication, good man management and quality. I suspect that my impression of industry was fairly similar to that of most people and about a hundred years out of date. The visits were certainly interesting and worthwhile and I feel that I have gained useful experience which I hope will be of use to others. A business studies or economics teacher, or even a physics teacher (if one can be found), would also find the experience of benefit.

Marianne Linford, a modern languages teacher at Highfield, reported on her visit to the John Lewis department store in Welwyn Garden City.

> As a sixth-form tutor and careers teacher I have learned sufficient about the retail trade to be able to counsel my students with some authority on this career. I have learned to appreciate that 'Retail is Detail' and that there are many more aspects than merely selling. I can now recommend retailing as a career to a wider range of students.

She sat in on recruitment interviews and also developed two schemes of work. The first was a problem-solving exercise based on the 'organization of merchandise', the second a decision-making exercise on 'display problems'. She came back happy to be working in a school rather than a shop: 'As a teacher with a young family, I now appreciate fully the flexibility my hours give me to combine two careers: that of mother and teacher.'

There are over 40 other teachers who left their classes for a flavour of how most of their pupils will eventually earn their livings. Of course not every teacher in Letchworth was keen on these placements. Some thought the approach condescending or irrelevant, others didn't want to consign their classes, particularly ones they were taking through the GCSE for the first time, to supply teachers. But Education 2000 can cope with dissent and scepticism for it was never intended as an orthodoxy to compel absolute adherence. Instead it offers teachers incentives. 'Maybe I have a touch of paranoia, but don't suggest the teachers have been bribed because I think this belittles the motivation of the teachers to the project,' says Richard Dix-Pincott. 'Education 2000 is not in the game of giving inducements. It simply seeks to try and implement proper professional practices as found in the better successful companies.' Whether these are bribes or proper professional practices the extra funding has nowhere been more obvious to outsiders than in the influx of computers. Very few Letchworth teachers rejected these potent symbols of modernity and, to help explain why, the next chapter will look at the importance vested in computers throughout British primary and secondary education.

Notes

1 *Education 2000: A Consultative Document on Hypotheses for Education in A.D. 2000* (1983). Cambridge: Cambridge University Press.
2 Howard, Ebenezer (1902) *Garden Cities of Tomorrow*, first published as *Tomorrow: A Peaceful Path to Reform* (1898).

5 Computers in British schools

At the Japanese School in west London, the one most favoured for the children of Japanese expatriates, there are no microcomputers in any of the classrooms. The teachers do not believe they fit into the main curriculum and they certainly wouldn't consider teaching computer studies. The study of the arcane mysteries of computer software and languages, and an understanding of the still more inscrutable business of what goes on inside the hardware, are seen as too specialized and grown up. They feel such studies don't belong in school and are as relevant to schoolchildren as the techniques of brain surgery, or the finer points of cost accounting. 'There are more important things to teach than computing,' says the school secretary, Mr Shigihara. 'Like sociology.'

Mr Shigihara's preference for teaching sociology rather than computing is a splendid reversal of Kenneth Baker's views; while sociology has been scorned and pushed to the educational margin, Mr Baker is the politician who has thrust computing to the centre of the educational agenda. During his first ministerial appointment, as the Minister for Information Technology attached to the Department of Trade, he introduced the £9 million Micros in Schools scheme to put a micro in every school in the land. That move, in 1982, was one of the most politically safe and uncontentious of the first Thatcher administration. The Labour party, which had accrued some political capital through the Microelectronics Applications Programme, was using rhetoric which could have come from Kenneth Baker's mouth.

In its 1985 'Jobs and Industry Campaign', the Labour party declared:

> Rapid technological change will affect most, if not all, of Britain's workforce. That is why our future prosperity depends on education and training of a high standard to meet new and unforeseen circumstances. We must seize the immense economic opportunities contained in advanced technologies by producing high tech goods and services. That means making a much bigger investment in high tech education and training.[1]

Here, at any rate, consensus ruled.

By the end of the Micros in Schools programme in 1984 there was indeed a micro in just about every British school. Other initiatives had followed. Most notable was the Microelectronics Education Programme (MEP), which ran from 1983 to 1986. In training thousands of teachers and spawning dozens of educational software packages it chalked up two other achievements. Firstly the MEP firmly established the principle of freely copiable cross-curricular software. The side effect of this was to haul computer education away from the dead end of concentrating on programming and from the distractions of bits and bytes and RAMS and ROMS. In fact the Letchworth schools' abandonment of information technology as a discrete subject owes much to the MEP example. Students who want to learn about programming get the chance but, unlike the ability to use word-processing packages, this skill is not automatically expected of them.

By 1987, according to Department of Education figures, the annual budget for computing in British schools amounted to £80 million. The magnetic effects of Mr Baker's technology-packed City Technology Colleges will stimulate demand still further but their influence will be minimal in relation to a spending frenzy which has only just begun. The Microelectronics Education Support Unit has recommended that 'a bare minimum' of £170 million must be found if computing demands implicit in the national curriculum are to be met. That will put at least eight micros into every primary school

47

and two per secondary core and foundation subject. Then there is all the equipment schools are going to buy to administer local financial management.

Nobody doubts the attachment of those in education's highest and lowest places to technology yet the question still lurks: are all these educational micros a good thing? Evidently Mr Baker was not entirely sure. Shortly before his elevation from Education Secretary to Conservative Party Chairman, he gave his approval for a £320,000 study into the impact of information technology on children's achievement. 'This project,' he declared, 'will greatly improve our knowledge of the impact that information technology is having across the curriculum and will help with the development of our information technology in schools strategy.'

One of the joint directors of the study, Dr Margaret Cox, is another techno-enthusiast, another person to have built a career on educational computing. As head of the Education Computing Unit at the Centre for Education Studies in London University's King's College, she is responsible for some of the most popular educational software packages. She certainly doesn't bother to project herself as the dispassionate academic researcher when she describes how Rice Farmer, a best-selling package from the college's 'Computer in the Curriculum' catalogue, can be of use in classrooms. In this package pupils play the part of a rice farmer. Amid droughts and deaths in the family, she explains, they have to grow the rice, market the crop, put some aside to eat and store some more for next year's seeds:

> The point about this is that there are no right and wrong answers. Role playing has them considering a host of financial and practical problems which would be difficult to do otherwise. This sort of simulation shows how computers can fill in the gaps where children often find difficulty in learning.

The belief from which she starts the research into the impact of information technology is that computers have changed the nature of learning by simulating what pupils used to observe in simplistic experiments or merely took on trust. Educational researchers have only just begun to take this technological change into account and Dr Cox recalls studies from the 1970s when those who first investigated the impact of information technology 'measured things which were irrelevant to the learning experience'. Her example is the common physics problem of looking at how a changed air resistance will alter the velocity of a falling object:

> The traditional method of measuring students' understanding would be to give them a problem to solve. Like tying a parachute to a stone. Traditional tests on problem-solving would assess students' descriptions of physical experiments which, clearly, for computer-based experiments is inadequate. Computer simulations enable students to explore the relationships between many different variables and one needs new techniques to explore their understanding of more complex relationships. This is the first such major assessment of its kind. Other research has tended to look at the way teachers work with computers rather than the impact of information technology on pupils.

I wondered if all this enthusiasm was the best qualification for one briefed to be objective in a search for evidence of the value of computers in schools. 'You can't measure the contribution information technology makes to learning if you don't understand it in the first place,' Dr Cox replied. 'Technology is developing skills nobody had ever anticipated.' Lest the educationists are not objective enough, the Department of Education has appointed the management consultants Peat Marwick McLintock as watchdogs and in three years' time a mixture of tabular material and written reports will give evidence on the importance of information technology to skills in 'problem-solving, exploration, information handling, decision-making and communications'. The academic, as opposed to the straightforwardly enthusiastic, side of Dr Cox looks forward to assessing 'consistent retained benefits ... what outcomes we can attribute to technology ... and which particular kinds of technology are most beneficial'. The report will be that of the convert preaching to the converted and while we can take it as given that school computing will emerge as a good thing, it will be fascinating to discover exactly how much of a good thing.

Meanwhile the technology in schools bandwagon rolls ever on; even Her Majesty's Inspectorate, a body not exactly renowned for outbursts of enthusiasm, is unequivocally up there with everybody else. In the HMI's *Curriculum Matters* series the inspectors said: 'Information technology, which is having a profound effect on pupils whose adult lives will be in the 21st century, should find a place in all subjects which are able to take advantage of the facility to store and process information and to generate further information.' In *The Curriculum from 5 to 16* HMI identified nine aspects of learning and experience as vital to a rounded education.[2] They are: aesthetic and creative; human and social; linguistic and literary; mathematical; moral; physical; scientific; spiritual; and technological.

In *Children Using Computers*[3] Anita Straker, whose beguiling literacy and numeracy packages such as Puff, Mathtalk and Martello Tower have made her one of the best-known names in educational software, uses HMI's categories of learning and experience to explain the impact that computers are making. In the aesthetic and creative area computers stimulate the processes of 'imagining, designing and inventing'. In the human and social area computers are valuable, asserts Mrs Straker, 'in the collection and study of evidence and opinion from the local environment, and in the role play which takes place when children are involved in a simulation activity'. Linguistic and literacy development are speeded along by computers which aid 'fluency and understanding in talking and reading and in the composition and refinement of writing'. Computers enhance maths teaching 'through the use of puzzles or strategy games, in the exploration of spatial relationships and patterns, in the solution of numerical problems and in the management and representation of statistical data'. She says the moral dimension of computing arises from 'questions about sharing time, taking turns, or the fair treatment of girls, in discussions about the use of computers to file information about people or the use of robots to replace people at work'. She sees the most direct curricular relevance of computers as in science subjects, where they assist 'the management and representation of information collected from observation, investigation or experiment and in the simulation of processes which would otherwise be too dangerous, too time-consuming or too expensive'.

Her final part to the fleshing out of computing's contribution to what HMI says every child must be is in the technological area. 'Computers,' she says, 'have an impact as a resource which can be used to bring about change or to exercise control over the environment.' There's nothing in this list of techno-logical potential about learning computing for its own sake, or about encouraging GCSE computer courses to prepare chil-dren for work as programmers. That echoes the position she reached at her previous job as primary head of the Microelec-tronics Programme. From her training adviser's desk at the Berkshire Local Education Authority, Anita Straker insists she is far more educationist than computer expert. Her words are worth noting carefully; as you read them it is more than likely that some child somewhere will be giving its all to one of her programs. The mystery of why there is nothing like a computer screen for holding a child's attention is one that Dr Cox's King's College researchers may be able to fathom.

Perhaps the major argument about micros in schools, now that their merit as cross-curricular and non-specialized tools is generally agreed on, concerns equal opportunities. An ingeni-ous line of argument has it that the introduction of computers to schools has actually inhibited the progress of women. The figures bear this out, for of the current intake of computer science graduates only 10 per cent are women, a deterioration from around a quarter in 1980. The problem begins at home where knock 'em dead computer games are marketed for the sort of little boys who used to read Dan Dare comics. Girls get elbowed off the valuable equipment; the toys for boys become machines for men and by A-level computer sciences, where the subject has remained in favour as a subject for those with the aptitude, only one in four candidates is female. Beyond the classroom, computing (although it is the world's youngest profession) has quickly evolved an elderly prejudice against women. Whereas women dominate the lowly paid and declining area of data processing – mindless keyboard bashing – they account for fewer than 5 per cent of data-processing managers.

It could be that society still adheres to ideas such as those of Nicholas Malebranche, the seventeenth-century philosopher who asserted that womanly intellects, with their 'soft and delicate brain fibres', are insufficient to penetrate scientific secrets. But it is more likely that a job in computing, which is secure, well paid and carries high status, is therefore, like other tasty professions, dominated by men. The Institute of Education's Professor Celia Hoyles edited a collection of essays, *Girls and Computers*,[4] in which several remedies are suggested. The main message in a series of case studies is that girls will participate as computing is bound up into the whole curriculum and not carved off as a separate subject area. Professor Hoyles urged 'the creation of more positive role models for girls', and she showed how far there is to go here by quoting an advertisement for the Acorn Archimedes computer where the slogan claimed that 'Even My Grandmother Can Use It'.

Her introduction began:

> It is a matter of grave concern that our culture is defining computers as pre-eminently male machines. Despite the fact that in everyday life computers are becoming ubiquitous, the use of the computer in education seems to be following the traditional lines of gender bias in society.

Every one of the book's contributors thought more computers would mean less discrimination, an observation which is borne out in Letchworth where I saw just as many girls as boys working on the computers.

Again the message is that more computers equal better education and, aside from the Japanese school in west London, there are few who would dissent from this educational orthodoxy. True, the Plymouth Brethren have found computers to be heretical, as machines that are built in an attempted likeness of the human mind. Their attempts to withdraw their children from lessons using computers have so far been resisted by the Department of Education and most local education authorities. In Letchworth every teacher I met, with one exception, had become a computer keenie. David Cursons, the head of science at St Christopher school, thinks computers are vastly overrated as a teaching aid. 'I don't believe in simulations,' he says. 'A simulation simply isn't an experiment. Science is the least liberal of subjects and I need to keep a tighter rein on classes than most of my colleagues. I'd prefer to rely on a demonstration rather than trusting what a programmer has decided to tell a computer to do.' He does occasionally use a micro for data-logging experiments, but prefers the Acorn BBC Micro he chose rather than the Research Machines ones the Education 2000 trust chose. Indeed, arguments about this or that micro are never far from any debate on educational technology although Mr Cursons was too indifferent to what he called 'all the technological rhetoric I've been hearing' to pursue it very far.

In the autumn of 1988 Martyn Harris put a memorable case against educational computing in his *Daily Telegraph* 'Odd Man Out' column. 'Computers in schools are a gimmick,' he wrote:

They are promoted by teachers because they are one of the few things the government will spend money on, and by the government because it is too ignorant and lazy to know better. In the early 1980s everyone suddenly started talking about the microchip, an obscure electronic component which had been around since the early 1970s, but had thrust itself into the public consciousness with the arrival of cheap personal computers. Headline writers struggled to find puns for the word 'chip' which did not involve fish, or old blocks or shoulders. TV documentaries began to talk of the 'microchip revolution' and newspapers to warn that Britain must not get left behind in the 'microchip race'. It was clearly one of those non-issues about which something had to be done. The government responded by appointing a non-person – the affable Heathite, Kenneth Baker – to the non-post of Minister for Information Technology. To everyone's surprise, Baker became a huge success, almost solely on the basis of his scheme to put a microcomputer into every school in the country. It cost practically nothing compared to any serious industrial investment and was highly visible. Every TV report on education featured the school computer, and every school put a picture of its micro in its prospectus. Somebody was bound to think of something to do with them eventually.

Having dismissed schools technology as mere political opportunism, Mr Harris trod old ground when he condemned the irrelevance of teaching 'computer literacy' and concluded:

> The other use for computers which the DES occasionally claims is as a teaching aid for subjects like maths or languages. There is some truth in this, but only where there is a computer for every child, or at least every two children, which would mean thirty times more computers than we already have. Given that computers, though cheap, will never be free, and given the enormous overhead needed in terms of maintenance and replacement, every five years or so, this level of provision is inconceivable.

Mr Harris's column lived up to its title: he proved to be the odd man out when his in-tray was filled with an unusually large number of letters from teachers who objected to what he had written. This proves that (a) there are a lot of teachers committed enough to computers in education to bother writing letters to newspapers; and (b) a lot of teachers still read *The Daily Telegraph*. What seemed inconceivable to Martyn Harris was precisely what John Abbott was conceiving: enough computers for every child to have regular turns at the keyboard. A speech he gave to the Confederation of British Industry in November 1987 was one he repeated many times for the Letchworth teachers.

Information technology is a powerful catalyst for change; it can transform the learning process. Let me take you into a detailed example of word processing. In the days of writing your own essays by longhand, did you ever consider rewriting an essay once marked by your teacher unless as a punishment? However shrewd and helpful the teacher's comments, did you put them directly to the test and actually work with the teacher to improve on your first effort? I didn't. My handwriting skills were too slow and copying out unnecessary text was a bore. Now think of a word processor. Many word processors. So many in a school that any child has access on demand. Think of teachers and pupils expecting that essays in any subject are handed in as word-processed text and then commented upon rather than marked. Then the text is returned so that the pupil, working with both the teacher's comments and the observations of friends, redrafts and resubmits the essay. Perhaps twice, maybe three times. And the eventual mark being a measure of the difference between the first and the final draft is not simply a rank ordering of pupil against pupil based on a handwritten first draft. Think about it. It is revolutionary and its implications are far-reaching.[5]

In making this speech Mr Abbott moved the technology in schools debate a stage further: his assertion was that computers are as vital to education as pencils, so they need to be nearly as numerous. What has happened since then is that the pupils' complete open access to computers which he'd imagined has been stymied for lack of money. The computer-to-pupil ratio stuck at 1:10 instead of the intended 1:6. Nonetheless, among the pupils in the early secondary years at whom the equipment has been directed, word processing has become a standard skill and the much worked-over word-processed essay has become the norm.

When Mr Abbott gave his speech to the CBI, the Letchworth schools had already started their bulk purchase of computers from a British manufacturer, Research Machines Ltd. I arrived early for my appointment with Research Machines' founder, Mike Fischer, and, since his headquarters in Oxford bans smoking, I waited outside in the car park. He got to the appointment bang on time, driving up in a Japanese imitation Range Rover. The account he gave of his business, which is one of the major suppliers of educational micros to British schools, owed much to precise timing and, it so happened, to doing things the Japanese way.

His initial piece of good timing was pure luck, for in 1976 Mr Fischer was the entrepreneur/boffin invited to attend a working party where the Berkshire Education Authority was considering making an educational micro. There was already the beginning of an educational micro market and with it, Mr Fischer could see, 'an unfulfilled demand' for a teacher-friendly box. He set out to fulfil this demand and lists the three steps which ensured the success of his first computer, the RML 380z: it was more reliable than its competitors; it didn't need a soldering iron to get it going; and it was easy to use.

Before talking about his computers, Mike Fischer sketched the way he had grown his business. During 1980, by which time his small company was working flat out producing 380z micros for schools in Havering, Birmingham and the Inner London Education Authority, Mr Fischer spent nearly half the year in Japan. Like Education 2000, he cannot overemphasize the importance of spending time away from the job. 'I realized many of the world's most excellent companies are Japanese,' he says. 'I worked on the assumption that if I knew a dragon's habits, I would know how to avoid it.' What he discovered was that many of the myths about Japanese success were unfounded and that 'everyone tried to ascribe that success to things they understood'. He says that though Japanese and British cultures are 'shockingly and profoundly different', the Japanese too had their strikes particularly in the late 1950s and early 1960s. So he refuses to explain Japanese productivity in terms of regimentation and mindless discipline. He says that a simple argument about investment in new technologies is insufficient too, especially in a country which has to import all its energy and raw materials. And he has no time for the argument that the Japanese declare lower profits. 'It is true,' he says, 'there are different accounting procedures but they are readily understood. What is important is that relative to inflation the Japanese pay the same interest rates.'

Eventually he identified two major differences. Japanese companies, like excellent companies elsewhere in the world, are run by boards which do not continually demand immediate profits and which moreover are conditioned to the idea of changing very rapidly: 'Anything a Japanese company is doing today,' he says, 'it realizes it ought to be doing differently in five years' time.' That means a certain level of speculative investment and the concentrating of resources on materials, project management and overall quality. 'Change' is the word Mr Fischer keeps repeating, almost like a mantra, and it is, of course, the same watchword which preoccupies so much of Education 2000's thinking.

Adaptability kept Research Machines afloat during its change-over from producing the 8-bit 380z and its immediate successor the 480z to the 16-bit Nimbus. Of the 32 micro manufacturers in business when Research Machines launched its first 380z on April Fool's Day 1977, only eight still survive and, Mr Fischer says, most of the failures occurred during the transition to more powerful microprocessors. In 1983 Research Machines' turnover, which sales of the 380z and 480z had sent to nearly £10 million, dipped. The changes weren't just in hardware, although there it was awkward and expensive enough. In 1983 nearly every micro manufacturer was following IBM into the MS DOS operating system and Research Machines went that way too, discarding the software expertise it had built up. 'Hair-raising times,' recalls Mike Fischer, with the smugness of one whose neatly coiffed head is the one at the top of a business which had a £50 million turnover in 1989.

Mr Fischer and his company have done well by paying heed to the doctrine of investing in constant change and Research Machines sees itself as a philosophical partner, as well as hardware supplier, to Education 2000. 'While the country spends fortunes on education,' says Mike Fischer, 'it invests little on explicit educational research and development. Education 2000 provided the best opportunity we saw to proto-type what might be achieved.' In the narrowest sense the

Research Machines commitment to Education 2000 has meant selling its computers at rock-bottom prices and then providing far above average technical support. In a broader sense Mike Fischer is concerned with what he calls 'lubricating change'.

He concedes that his computers, and the same would apply to those from many other manufacturers, are merely one of the lubricants:

> Computers provide excitement and focus. But fundamentally Education 2000's objectives are not technical. They are prototyping issues and approaches to how students might be able to contribute to and enjoy a changing society. From my experience of Japan, I have learnt that new ideas need new techniques and my observation of what is happening in Letchworth is that, at the very least, teachers and pupils are extremely well motivated. There is still a long way to go but they are developing a vocabulary for issues relating to change.

Mike Fischer comes over every bit as idealistic and full of hope as John Abbott and concluded, 'What is lacking in the West is an understanding that management of change is an explicit discipline; Education 2000 is making a contribution to remedying that deficit.'

Notes

1 *Labour's Jobs and Industry Campaign* (1985). Labour Party/TUC Paper.
2 HMI (1985) *The Curriculum from 5 to 16* (Curriculum Matters no. 2). London: HMSO.
3 Straker, Anita (1989) *Children Using Computers*. Oxford: Blackwell Education.
4 Hoyles, Celia (ed.) (1988) *Girls and Computers*. London: Institute of Education.
5 Abbott, John (1987) 'Industry/schools partnership for excellence.' Speech at the CBI National Conference.

6 Computers in Letchworth schools 'Information technology as the means'

When Kenneth Baker visited Letchworth on 13 April 1988 he approved of what he found in the schools he toured. A few days later, the visit still fresh in his mind, he addressed delegates to a conference on New Technology for Better Schools:

> I have just visited a project in Letchworth for Education 2000, which has taken the schools in Letchworth together and has promoted this concept of the schools working together, providing a lot of extra equipment and doing it [i.e. information technology] across the curriculum, and it was very impressive indeed. So impressive that they have virtually dropped separate computer studies ... that should be the objective of what we are striving for in the course of the next five to ten years.

Thus Education 2000 had earned the highest approval for its bold aim of using computers to refashion the curriculum. The Secretary of State for Education, no less, had at least partly endorsed it as a model for the future. The 'concept of schools working together', particularly in the provision of computers, is one that had strong appeal to Mr Baker, who later that year told teachers:

> We need more equipment, better software, more trained staff and more support services. I expect to see local education authorities co-operating and forming consortium arrangements with other LEAs so that together they can provide better coverage than will be possible for a single LEA working alone.

Unparalleled amounts of equipment and trained staff and support services and overall co-operation was precisely what Mr Baker had witnessed in Letchworth. Other parts of British education have realized the economies of scale that result from organizing information technology centrally. The prime example is the old Inner London Education Authority's Inner London Education Computing Centre. ILECC, with its staff of 40 and annual budget of £750,000, is the country's biggest source of advice on computers in teaching and, aside from the support it gives to London's teachers, is big enough to have written much software. The Smile mathematics packages and the Allwrite multilingual word-processing package are among the best-known results of this work.

Hertfordshire schools have had a similar cross-authority computing body for a long time. Two decades ago, in 1969, the Advisory Unit for Computer Based Education (AUCBE) was set up in Hatfield. Under the directorship of Dr Bill Tagg, AUCBE has provided in-service training, technical advice and, like ILECC, has also become an educational software house. Its training role was curtailed in 1987 when the Hertfordshire County Council got a DES Educational Support Grant to implement information technology across the curriculum. The curtailment of AUCBE's training brief has been the subject of much concern within Education 2000 and throughout the county at large. AUCBE and Bill Tagg have been close friends of Education 2000 and the project has been saddened to see how AUCBE has become isolated from the authority's advisory services. It goes to show that computers are not always a recipe for educational consensus.

While Dr Bill Tagg has provided Education 2000 with consultancy help, Nick Peace has been responsible for the day-to-day help and maintenance that inevitably came with the introduction of all the Letchworth school computers. Until 1982 Mr Peace taught mathematics and computer studies and was head of computer studies at the John Bunyan School in Bedford. Then he worked for John Abbott as head of the Open Terminal technology centre in Stevenage. He is one of those teachers who absorb finer details of the computer culture as if by osmosis. He's a diplomat too and any conversation with him in his technology-crammed attic office at the Letchworth Garden City Corporation's headquarters is bound to be interrupted by telephoned requests for help. 'Have you turned the printer on?' he asks, without a trace of scorn in his voice. This is sometimes enough, but on other occasions he'll pack his doctor's bag of floppy discs and screwdrivers and visit immediately, to defuse all panic.

Mr Peace joined Education 2000 in April 1986 and remained in his post as information technology manager even after the trust's funding dried up. In what must be an unprecedented financial arrangement, his deputy head's salary is shared between the six schools. It is a measure both of his value and of the schools' commitment to their computer programmes that the private and state sectors have worked so closely together and have continued, out of their own budgets, to fund such a staff member. A strong point in favour of the consensual worth of computing in schools, Nick Peace's appointment exemplifies the fact that, as the trust intended, community activity has been a stimulus to change. Information technology has been the means. 'The fundamental aim of this information technology component,' said the trust's manifesto, 'is to exploit the power of information technology, on a scale not previously attempted in schools, to enrich, extend and transform current curriculum practice in both teaching and learning.'[1] The teachers agreed and time and again they stress that computers are a means to an end. 'Computers,' says St Christopher's second deputy head, Julian Cottenden, 'are the most obvious things which outsiders can see but in an important sense they are secondary. Their subliminal effect has been to engender closeness and community.' That sense of a common purpose is all the more remarkable for having come about during a tumultuous time for teachers so an account of the Letchworth schools' technological progress can't simply be one of counting in the computers.

In the months before Nick Peace's appointment the six Letchworth headteachers had been attending a meeting every Friday. They had had much to discuss, some of it nothing to do with the Education 2000 plans which had brought them together. In September 1985 the teachers' pay dispute had begun with its ban on extra-curricular activities. As elsewhere in British education, morale dropped; GCSE was looming; Letchworth was one of the first phase of the Technical and Vocational Education Initiative extensions and, as a taster of what was to come, each of the four state schools was installing 16-station Research Machines Nimbus networks.

Stevenage is one of the pilot TVEI towns and both Nick Peace and John Abbott had been heartily involved with it before they arrived in Letchworth. TVEI, which later on was taken up by the four state schools in Letchworth, sits in uneasy counterpoint to Education 2000; it too was using technology to mould a new curriculum and it too wanted to bring schools and community together though in a far more directly vocational way than Education 2000 envisaged. TVEI differed in being far more explicitly designed to defuse local authority power. It was, in effect, a back-door move towards a national curriculum and its funds came not from the Department of Education but from Lord Young's Manpower Services Commission. As the paymaster of this particular scheme the MSC was able to sidestep local authorities and exercise control over the content and form of its mixture of vocational education and job-related training.

In some respects Education 2000 has taken the £1.2 billion national TVEI project and written it more boldly. Instead of applying to 14- to 18-year-olds, it is for 11-plus and provides schools with the funds for more computers and more teachers. Where Fearnhill, in crude terms, got 40 hours INSET via TVEI, it had four extra teachers through Education 2000. However, the Education 2000 emphasis, despite the more direct backing from industry, is less directly vocational. 'Vocational?' queried a couple of teachers at Highfield. Stern looks. 'That is not our function. We're giving a general education in preparation for a computer-literate world. I don't see it as any more vocational than maths or writing.'

By the time of Nick Peace's appointment, the headteachers had started to develop a separate Education 2000 computing strategy. On the principle of priming the staff before installing the systems, each head nominated a technologized staff member to act as information technology co-ordinator. They were drawn from many disciplines and the team Mr Peace was to work closely with over the next years was: Roy Unsworth, a mathematics teacher from Fearnhill; Rosemary Ryden, a music teacher from Highfield; Pat Wisby, a mathematics teacher from Norton; Anthony Harris, a mathematics teacher from St Christopher; Soo Pope, a home economics teacher from St Francis; and Bill Murphy, a geography teacher from Willian. From September 1986 they had release time built into their time-tables, allowing them to meet every week for two hours. None from this cross-curricular group was a technological virgin although Nick Peace had his work cut out to make them skilled enough to take charge of their colleagues' technology training.

The plan to which they were central envisaged a two-year phase during which 25 extra staff would be appointed throughout the Letchworth schools to enhance staffing by 10 per cent. This would enable every member of staff to be released from normal teaching for, on average, the equivalent of 40 days. These 40 days were to be taken in various units of single days to a whole week but, they had to bear in mind, 'these were not to be spasmodic or unrelated'. On any one school day, 25 staff were to be involved in training courses for a total of 10,000 separate day units. As it turned out lack of money meant these projections were revised down to about 8 per cent, typically two and a half teachers per school, and 90 per cent was delivered within the structure of the timetable. Technology was to be the catalyst in this massive upgrading of INSET though, unlike much traditional INSET, the training was centred in the schools. Perhaps the most motivating part for the teachers was that they were encouraged to take new computers home. This bold, if obvious, idea began that September and continued for two terms; the automatic freedom to learn about computers away from the glare of a classroom or staff-room is another important ingredient of the Education 2000 mixture.

Take-home computers and time to consider how to adapt teaching techniques to the technology were the carrots Letchworth teachers got at a time when many sticks were flying. In November the pay dispute had been forced to an unhappy conclusion, with the withdrawal of union negotiating rights. The much-resented Education Reform White Paper was published in December. The following May saw the Conservative election manifesto proving, with a vengeance, that 'something was going to be done' about what had become 'the education problem'. In it were proposals for the national core curriculum and the increased central control that implied, in addition to plans for schools opting out of local authority control, increased parental choice and the local management of schools. While teachers could agree that this was good in parts, they also felt demoralized and under threat. Yet two years into the project, the trust was able to report that the

> information technology programme has involved about two thirds of the teachers in the Inset activities and directly the children in the second year of the school for two years and in the first year for one. In reality the impact has been on the whole school with most of the staff and young people actively involved in some way with the technology. The horizon of staff involved in the curriculum areas tend to have been raised and the technology appears to provide the focus for more cross-curricular development.[2]

This is to jump forward in time. Back in 1986, the fact that the staff had taken home Research Machine Nimbus micros showed that at least one Great Debate had been resolved. The headteachers had been discussing what technology to use since their first meetings in September 1985. By this time Nimbus micros were about to be installed as part of TVEI, so Research Machines was always a front runner. But other educational micros were also under consideration. The stakes were high. At the very least a contract for £500,000 was in the offing and, as Letchworth was intended to be an example for the rest of the country, even bigger sales could be anticipated later on. In March four contenders were being considered: Research Machines, a consortium of Amstrad, ICL and STC, Apricot and IBM. According to Richard Dix-Pincott:

> Apricot was only interested in providing hardware without further involvement; whereas IBM was heavy on ideas but was not clear about what it would be able to deliver. The Amstrad/ICL/STC consortium came up with a very interesting package but it was not sufficient to challenge Research Machines which not only offered excellent hardware and commercial standard software but an educational vision for the future matched by a promise of high-quality technical support.

Nick Peace, a Research Machines man from his days at the Stevenage Open Terminal centre, joined at the same time as the Spicer and Pegler management consultancy agreed to conduct an 'implementation plan'. In May, when Kenneth Baker got his education post, trustees, headteachers, IT co-ordinators and manufacturers' representatives met for a conference at the Grosvenor Hotel in London. This was also the first time that funding difficulties became publicly apparent but it didn't stop a number of important decisions being ratified. The conference confirmed that while hardware was to be purchased centrally by the trust from a single manufacturer, it would be left to the schools to decide where to put it and, with the active participation of the information technology co-ordinators and other staff members, what it was used for. This became known as 'encouraging ownership'. It was also confirmed that the computers would be strung together in networks across the schools rather than installed in isolation in separate classrooms. They all but decided to divide the computers on a pro rata basis according to the number of teachers rather than pupils, which would have favoured the independent schools with their smaller classes. John Abbott's predilection for word processing as the prime computing skill for all pupils was underscored and a strong preference for 'mouse'-controlled screens was expressed.

A mouse is a palm-sized device with a large ball bearing in its base which rolls on the surface of a desk and registers a corresponding pointer on the computer screen. The benefit of a mouse is both to make first use of a computer easy for children who might be intimidated by a QWERTY keyboard, and to make it quicker for anybody else. It should be mentioned that, such is the children's respect for the computers, vandalism is minimal. There is, according to Nick Peace, one blemish on a happy record. Some children prise open the mouse backs to extract the ball bearings and have created a little black market in these.

A month after the Grosvenor Hotel conference Research Machines won the contract. It wasn't the cheapest possible option, but there were three reasons why Mr Peace favoured the Oxfordshire company that has founded its success on selling educational computers. First, its computers 'are always given an upgrade path'. He'd been in the business long enough to know that the first computer anybody buys is never ever big enough and as the networks grew he was glad he'd remembered this computer truism. Second, Research Machines had long been committed to networking its computers. The advantage for schools is that networked terminals are cheaper than stand-alone ones as they rely on a single storage system and a limited number of printers. Many schools had been persuaded by this logic since the first 480z Chain network was sold in the early 1980s but the 70 terminal networks being discussed in Letchworth were larger than Research Machines had put into any other school.

The disadvantage with networks is that their management grows in complexity with their size. From the outset Research Machines had defined Letchworth as a test site and therefore pledged greater support to its schools than is usual. That pledge was called on during the 1988 school year when the Letchworth networks demanded attention from a Research Machines engineer for two days a week. One of the lessons its boss Mike Fischer has learnt is that his company must supply technical support with its bigger networks and as a result he is recruiting technical support engineers to cope with the day when many educational networks have '60 or 100 or 200 work stations'. His engineers have used Letchworth in their development of Research Machines' most recent Net 3 network-control software which concentrates on improvements in speed, general ease of management and tighter security so that clever fourth-formers can't gatecrash the operating software.

Mr Peace's glowing recommendation of Research Machines echoes that of Richard Dix-Pincott. 'They sold us far more than just boxes,' he says. 'We have had the highest levels of technical support from them.' So, everybody's happy though it must be said that Letchworth's favoured status as a pilot scheme has guaranteed it the kind of perfect friendship with a manufacturer which other schools would be foolish to expect.

The third reason Nick Peace favours Research Machines, and it is one which predisposes many other teachers towards the company, is the software it supplies free of charge with its networks. The company's 'bundled software', which is all the more useful for including packages that are widely used in business and commerce, is what marks it out from the competition. By hyping up 'the strategic marketing opportunity of the century' Mike Fischer was able to persuade software houses virtually to give away their software so that schools buying RM Net network servers have a range of commercial and educational software within the price. From the huge American firm Microsoft there is Word for word processing, the Excel database management package, Multiplan for spreadsheets and Windows which is a means to link various application programs together. Additionally there is Write, Quest, PC Paintbrush, Basic, Pascal, Logo, RM CAD, Dataease and the Touch 'n Go typing tutor.

To illustrate the rule that what comes with the first computer is never enough, the information technology co-ordinator at Norton School pulled out the 35 extra packages her school has purchased. Pat Wisby described how, from the early days when she'd taken the first fifteen staff for a double period of

Inset each week, staff resistance to computers had crumbled. The English department had soon demanded Front Page Extra, a desk-top publishing package. From her files she took out class-produced magazines to add to my collection of other examples from Fearnhill and St Christopher. The geography department had bought in Plate Tectonics, which simulates geological developments; the maths department wanted more and better spreadsheets; and by popular demand from the children she bought the ILECC Smile packages of brilliant little educational games where, for example, darts games are mocked up and the scores are only registered if the mental arithmetic is done correctly.

It is with some pride that Pat Wisby explains how the computers have infiltrated the school. While the Nimbus hardware she got had been predetermined by the trust's choice for bulk purchase discounts and ease of administration, the exact arrangement of where they went was left to the schools. Norton School comprises several buildings and the distance between them would have created problems if every machine were to be linked. Of all the Letchworth schools Norton has the most stand-alone machines; discrete single systems went to the history, geography, home economics, maths and art departments, and the library, school office, headmaster and sixth-form common room each had a machine as well. Small clustered networks, which don't need an extra machine operating as a file server, went to maths, craft design and technology, special needs, 'resources' and the English workroom. Two larger networks, each with its own file server and 60-megabyte storage unit, went into rooms dubbed IT1 and IT2.

These two larger networks are now being lashed together and while we talked Pat Wisby took a phone call and jotted down some deep techno advice from one of the other IT co-ordinators. 'Yes, of course all the IT co-ordinators have phones in their offices,' she said after the call. 'And no, I don't see this as any kind of concession; a phone is absolutely vital for our work.' True enough, but something which most teachers can't yet take for granted; for the most part they can't even use the photocopiers to which all the Letchworth teachers seemed to have ready access.

In his office Nick Peace ran through the other networks. 'We've gathered a variety of experience,' he said. 'It's important that we haven't got a uniform arrangement.' Fearnhill, the largest school, has 70 terminals while St Francis, the smallest, has 25 on a single network. He lapses into gobbledegook, saying how St Christopher is 'in the process of upgrading from a single LAN [Local Area Network] with an AX and going over to a twin server with a dual LAN'. His trouble-shooting role is easier to understand. He's had to persuade the Fearnhill teachers that their system doesn't have a virus. At Norton they'd had a hacking problem and some unidentified but resourceful pupils had been corrupting the control software. 'They've been finding holes through the Word package and getting in that way,' he explains. 'We've patched it up for the moment and when Research Machines delivers Net 3 [which was designed with exactly this sort of adolescent sabotage in mind], we'll be secure again. St Christopher is the worst place for this as the boarders have more time.' All in a day's work for a town's information technology manager.

Nick Peace also administers a host of other technology such as satellite dishes, video cameras, Prestel and Teletel receivers and music synthesizers: more of these later. The latest addition to Letchworth's rich technological mix is a £150,000 Micro Vax electronic conferencing system donated by Digital Equipment. Messages pass down British Telecom lines (which BT has declined to donate) between the six schools, the Letchworth Garden City office and, to extend the co-operation out of town, to the North Herts College Campus in Letchworth. A further £150,000 has been donated by Digital, which will extend the conferencing system to the North Herts College Hitchin Campus and to the secondary schools in Hitchin and neighbouring towns. Over 400 people have already logged on at the 45 terminals Digital provided to a range of 30 or so conferences with titles such as Gossip, Scholar, Heads, Craftie, Dickens and Icthus. Gossip is for everyone and, scrolling

69

through the record of the messages passed, one of its levelling oddities is that it is impossible to tell whether a teacher or a pupil has made a particular entry. Scholar is limited to students and is moderated by one of the sixth-formers. Heads is a closed conference for private communication by the headteachers and project directors, Craftie for craft design technology teachers, Dickens for those involved with library projects and Icthus for religious education teachers in the curriculum development groups.

Nick Peace scrolls through pages of on-screen messages giving advice on calculus and exits to another conference arranging a rock-climbing expedition in North Wales. So far teachers have used it less than the pupils who, under all sorts of weird pseudonyms, log into discussions which range from the Pons-Fleichman cold fusion experiments to the latest in cross-town computer dating services. 'The potential of this facility is only barely being appreciated, even for those acquainted with such technology', is the line the trust is taking. Hilary Sepahy, a secondee from the North Herts College, was appointed at the beginning of the 1989 term to 'develop the learning aspects of electronic conferencing and to make it function as a perfectly normal part of the educational process'.

In the technological sense Letchworth's schools, with their 311 Nimbus microcomputers and 45 Micro Vax conference terminals, are the most privileged in the country (See Appendix 4). Its computer-to-pupil ratio is 1:10 as opposed to the average of one per 32 pupils reported in a Department of Education and Science statistical bulletin during Summer 1989.[3] In addition to the extra computers, there has been extra time for the teachers, but, as we saw in Chapter 2, the privileges have cost only £105 per pupil per year. Has it been money well spent?

Richard Dix-Pincott is convinced of the benefits that Education 2000 and the computers have brought:

The use of computers has created a different model to traditional education. Relationships between staff and pupils have become less formal. Instead of the teacher confronting pupils with a fixed body of information in the old didactic way, we're offering self-supported study, resource-based skills and an inner structured environment. Computers help us propagate a message to the children that they are the ones who are ultimately responsible for their learning. Computers epitomize this transition; their databases hold more than a teacher's mind ever could; and their operation often involves the teacher relying on a pupil's superior knowledge. The moment teachers say they are not the sole source of information, things are bound to change.

All this was by way of explaining the Education 2000 slogan 'From teaching to learning', a phrase also expanded on in the project's 1989 annual report. 'One of our objectives,' it says, 'is to enable the young person to cultivate the capability to learn ... to accept guidance from his or her teacher in the pursuance of knowledge, but to learn how to learn and to go on doing so for a life time.'[2] The 'teaching to learning' process which lies at the project's heart was the chief topic to emerge from a project conference at Trinity College, Cambridge, in September 1988. It was agreed there that the computing did indeed 'provide the basis of teaching to learning right across the curriculum' and, less helpfully, it was also agreed that this 'process is elusive and difficult to explain and harder still to do'.

Education 2000's motto, 'From teaching to learning', has already spread far beyond Letchworth. The TVEI Training Agency, as part of its policy to 'promote flexible learning', asked the Education 2000 trust to mount a national conference which met in May 1989 (see Appendix 5). The resulting conference report owed more to Education 2000 ideals than it did to the vocational versions of education which originally breathed life into TVEI.[4] In the chairman's concluding remarks George Tolley, the higher education adviser at the Training Agency, outlined four national needs, and did so in language which could have been lifted straight from documents about the Letchworth experiment.

Mr Tolley's four points were: first, to redefine and restate

71

the professionalism of tutors [a word the conference substituted for teachers] and better appreciate the changing roles of schools in themselves and their communities; second, to agree what structures and mechanisms to develop and when and how to develop them; third, to get local responses so that each community should define what it wants from its schools and then fully support them; and fourth, to increase the level of resources to energize the fast-changing nature of schools. 'The resources,' said George Tolley, 'include time and information technology systems.' More time. More technology. This sounds very like Education 2000.

Notes

1 *Education 2000: A Consultative Document on Hypotheses for Education in A.D.2000* (1983). Cambridge: Cambridge University Press.
2 *Annual Report* (1989) Education 2000.
3 *Statistical Bulletin* (July 1989). London: DES.
4 *From Teaching to Learning: A First Consultation Report* (1989). HMSO under contract to the DES Training Agency.

7 The Letchworth classrooms 'Curriculum development as the result'

The Westfield conference agreed that what should be taught in schools 'should meet the needs of those, of all aptitudes, who will grow up in the coming decades of great technological development yet in a national society which adheres to traditional values'. This was soon translated as 'curriculum development'.

John Sayer, an Education 2000 trustee until 1989 and one of the Westfield delegates, thinks 'probably it is time to stop using the word curriculum . . . curriculum, in fact, has come to mean education, whilst the word education is increasingly and wrongly used to describe either the system which delivers it or the study of education.' He wrote this in 1984, when he was head of the Banbury Comprehensive, in his book *What Future for Secondary Schools?*.[1] He mentioned Education 2000 just once, and concluded his chapter entitled 'The Mirage of Curriculum' by condemning 'the ossified formal programme which forms only one part of the responsibilities of teaching'. Mr Sayer recommended that

> the whole curriculum offered through school, is now to be seen in the context of other learning opportunities, through existing media and new technologies which for certain purposes can replace the classroom . . . school education could make sense in the future only if its whole contribution could be considered in the context of all localised learning opportunities.

Elsewhere there were many other similarly resounding words drawn from a range of discontent. Everybody who was anybody in education, in a continuation of James Callaghan's

Great Debate, was insisting that something must be done. The 1985 White Paper, *Better Schools*,[2] proposed that if there were a broad agreement between the education service and other interested parties on the objectives and content of the school curriculum, two things would follow. First, 'it would be clear what tasks society expects our schools to accomplish. The schools' performance could then be more fairly judged against agreed expectations about these tasks.' And second, 'it would mean parents, employers and public would have a closer understanding of the purposes for which they are being asked to support the work of the schools in achieving common aims'.

Two years earlier, in 1983, Her Majesty's Inspectorate published *Red Book Three, Curricula 11–16; Towards a Statement of Entitlement*.[3] They'd worked at this for six years and a few extracts can be used to give wider context to the Education 2000 agenda. 'The reshaping of the secondary curriculum may best be achieved by discussions which include people outside as well as within the schools,' said HMI. 'All those concerned with education have a responsibility to voice their perceptions of what an appropriate curriculum might be.'

During his time as Secretary of State for Education, Keith Joseph had called on all local education authorities in England and Wales to reveal their arrangements for the school curriculum. In a comment which can, with a degree of imagination, be taken as a prediction of both the national curriculum and of Education 2000, the Department of Education and Science's *Planning the Curriculum as a Whole* had this to say:

> Today changes are gathering momentum, and we have to try to forecast the kind of society our children will enter when they leave school. Many, perhaps the majority, will have to be prepared for major changes of life style. As society becomes freer, more responsibility is placed on its individual members. These considerations must be in our minds when we plan our organisation and the work we are going to present. Never has it been more important that children develop self-discipline, imagination, an ability to think, to ask questions and to assess answers, to develop resourcefulness and independence.[4]

In its response to these central demands for curriculum reappraisal, the Hertfordshire County Council's *Curriculum Policy for Schools* stated: 'In planning and reviewing their curricula, schools should look beyond their traditionally titled subjects, or disciplines, to the areas of experience and knowledge which they may help to develop.'[5] Elsewhere in Hertfordshire John Abbott was on his secondment at work on a paper, 'Towards a secondary curriculum appropriate for the year 2000', which was to serve as one of the Letchworth blue prints. His work echoed phrases which were gaining broader and broader currency:

> There is an overriding need to plan the curriculum as a single entity, rather than treat it as a number of separate disciplines, with clear overall objectives expressed in terms of skills, attitudes, concepts and knowledge. This planning must incorporate the schools' full response to needs of the pupils ... the curricular (formal and informal) and the extra curricula.[6]

He went on to suggest how a range of initiatives could be drawn together into a coherent programme.

Before John Abbott had a formal attachment to Education 2000, the rather vague prescription for 'curriculum development' was cohering into a desire to 'shift away from subject-specific teacher instruction towards effective learning strategies for the individual, supported by exploiting the full potential of information technologies'.[7] This formula owed much to Ray Dalton, the former principal lecturer in education at Cambridge University's Homerton College who became the project's educational consultant and, in a less official way, mentor to John Abbott. From the beginning Mr Dalton was determined to avoid the polemic which was gathering around the national debate on the curriculum. Put at its simplest, the debate pushes people into one of two camps. Faction one puts an emphasis on knowledge and seeks to create order by describing the discrete bits of subjects which should be taught. Faction two is less emphatic about subject areas and says it is more important for teachers to concentrate on concepts, attitudes, skills and knowledge. At the moment the national curriculum has put faction one in the ascendant, but to restrict a consideration of what has happened in Letchworth's classrooms to the terms of this dispute would be to leave its consensual aims far behind.

Curriculum development, the third strand of Education 2000's aims, was the trickiest to put into practice and the curriculum reappraisal was potentially the most wobbly and contentious plank of the whole philosophy. It was inextricably bound up with statutory directives about preparing pupils for public examinations, with tie-ins to schemes such as TVEI and the huge changes being wrought by the national curriculum which was announced in May 1987. Having defined 'community activity as the stimulus and information technology as the means' the project hoped for 'curriculum development as the result. . .'. Mr Dalton says that the way in which the curriculum groups were intended to develop was deliberately left less defined than for the community or information technology groups. As he explains:

> The project was always an exploration and curriculum development was a part of that exploration. There was no attempt at the start to direct the nature of the programme because at root it was an attempt to bring teachers together as an educational community. They had to recognize developments and claim ownership because the aim was to involve every teacher in the town.

Mr Dalton wanted to steer Education 2000's efforts towards generating changes from within the system in a 'bottom up' teacher-directed shift rather than a 'top down' imposition of change. 'Teacher empowerment' is the phrase of a man who, in a quietly understated way, makes it his business to undermine the harsher dogmas of the 1980s.

In the estimation of Richard Dix-Pincott, the teachers' efforts at curriculum exploration have been a success. 'Education 2000,' he told me whilst he was still the acting head at Fearnhill, 'is a development from within which organically affects the service in a way not possible by grafting on patterns from the outside.' He'd been showing me a rack of mahogany racing cars, the best of which were well-carved Formula-One-style models complete with go-faster stripes, while the worst looked like bricks on wheels. The headmaster ran one of the model cars up and down a bench top and recalled that he'd spent a year making a teapot stand when he was at school; his first-years had spent a term on their cars. I said it had taken me a school year to make a pair of stilts and we agreed that in Letchworth things were much better nowadays. This familiar comparison between one's own schooling and what is now occurring decades later can make a teacher's job very hard, because recollection of half-remembered disgruntlement is a tenuous basis for an educational assessment. But a comparison of my own schooling and what I found in Letchworth excited me and, along with Mr Dix-Pincott's feeble schoolboy woodwork achievements, I recalled John Abbott's account about his own boredom as a schoolboy.

They are not saying schooling was rotten in the past, nor that it is utterly deficient now. However, implicit in what many Education 2000 proponents say are criticisms of an old and creaky education system and, spoken more softly, of many current initiatives. By comparison with the educational aims of Education 2000, those of the new GCSE are sometimes cast as little better than a remodelled GCE O-level, branding many children as failures, while the national curriculum is seen as limiting. Brandishing the car as a kind of totem, Mr Dix-Pincott laughed at the teaching practice student whose hand-written worksheets were rejected as too crude by the computer-wise pupils.

I took those cars as a clear example of an approach which the cloudy Education 2000 jargon defines as 'functional literacy for all and the ability to feel comfortable amidst the changes of a highly technological democratic society'. Not that this would mean much to the first-years who had started the project using the Word word-processing package on their Nimbus micros to write a design brief. They switched to PC Paint and drew up to six racing car profiles squeezed on one screen; then the favoured design was enlarged and printed out as a template. Before the models were carved and stained the most nifty of the pupils tipped the designs into the three-dimensional, using the Compass Designer software package. Hands then stopped shuffling the mouse and pattering at the keyboards, to cut the wood but the project didn't finish there; pupils returned to the computers to call up the Multiplan financial modelling package. Labour was generously costed at 75 pence per hour so that, including the cost of the materials, the finished products worked out at £10 each.

'Worth it at twice the price,' said Danny Walton, the Fearnhill craft design and technology teacher. I wondered if the computers were worth it too. 'Of course they are,' he replied to this heretical query:

> They're tools like a Pritt Stick or a saw and they're about as expensive as the vacuum formers and line benders in the workshops next door. The computers also mean I can work alongside students more. Everyone is more productive and the multi-disciplinary way I can teach now involves all departments.

Brian Bedford, head of craft, design and technology (CDT) at Norton, used to be an old-style woodwork teacher but, as he approaches the end of his career, he will bow out an Education 2000 convert. 'At first I couldn't see any possible use for computers,' he says. 'I was swayed when I saw even the weaker pupils could get good-looking hard copy of their design work.' He became enthused by weekly meetings with his counterparts from other schools, the demonstrations from software manufacturers, the visits to companies such as British Aerospace and his growing computing skills. 'Not that I'm an expert,' he says. 'I often have to rely on clever pupils to help me out.' With his talk of PC Paint, Compass Designer Autodraft 2, In-a-Vision and the virtues of laser printing he sounds pretty much of an expert now.

Mr Bedford and Mr Walton were part of the CDT curricular group which met once a week from September 1987. The group was unanimous in its interest in computer aided design and the major thrust of its work was to discover how computers could help put new ideas into practice. Over two years later the result is technology-packed workshops which children clamour to use outside the timetable. The first curriculum groups started to meet at the same time as the community and information technology groups. The CDT group, by all accounts the most tightly knit of the curriculum groups, pioneered a mechanism of bidding for resources where the rules for getting an allocation of time outside the classroom plus resources to buy kit were that proposals had to be both cross-curricular and cross-school. Thus the CDT teachers, following ideas that had developed nationally, bridged the gap between themselves and the science departments by putting in successful bids for control technology kit. A year later Steve Taylor, the Norton deputy head who had chaired the CDT meetings, started on a half-time secondment as curriculum co-ordinator to look after a staff enhancement model which followed a pattern something like this:

Designation	*School enhancement*
IT co-ordinator	0.5
computer network manager	0.25
science co-ordinator	0.1 each (=0.3)
home economics co-ordinator	0.1 each (=0.3)
modern languages co-ordinator	0.1 each (=0.3)
CDT development	0.1 (in five schools)
library project	0.5 (in two schools)
liaison and evaluation	0.1 each (=0.2)
other teacher support	1.2 (approx.)

Thus staff enhancement was initially provided to library, craft design technology, science, home economics and languages. The first four benefited from some allocation within the time-table while modern languages relied on supply teachers. Although common timetabling was possible for the craft design technology group, a time in lieu model was more commonly used with teachers meeting after school in 'twilight time'. This is no simple model and was arrived at after lengthy negotiation. The results impressed teachers in other disciplines enough for them to establish further inter-school groups in special needs, religious education, music, video and control technology. It gave ten groups in all, five of them unplanned in Education 2000's original Letchworth proposals, and the 1988 annual report sounded a satisfied note when it recorded that over 50 teachers were meeting regularly:

> Taking into account their feedback to departmental colleagues in the schools, it is likely that over 120 teachers in Letchworth are being influenced through this curriculum activity, some 50 per cent of the total establishment. This figure rises even higher almost to 100 per cent in one or two schools, if staff involved in information technology developments are also included.

To summarize, the ten parts of curriculum development that evolved are:

1 Craft, design technology (computer aided design)
2 Science (resource-based learning)
3 Home economics (resource-based learning)
4 Modern languages (technological developments)
5 Special needs (support Inset and software)
6 Religious education (resource development; world faiths theme)
7 Music (curriculum co-ordination and computer aided composition)
8 Video camera (cross-curricular use of camcorder technology)
9 Control (control technology across craft design technology, information technology and science)
10 Libraries

What follows is a glance at each one of these areas, with the exceptions of the CDT group which has already been covered and the Letchworth school libraries, which deserve a short chapter to themselves.

Science teachers from all the Letchworth schools, often with county advisory staff present, took part in a series of fortnightly meetings to discuss curriculum reappraisal and standardization. Some 'confusion as to the methodology and purpose of the project' was reported and eventually ascribed to the group's mixture of heads of department and junior staff. 'There was a lot of navel contemplation going on,' complained one head of department, and another interpretation of the confusion was that the traditionalists who relied on scientific demonstration clashed with the modernists who favoured 'more adventurous discovery models'.

In the end the group reported it 'wished to develop a module, based on supported self-study and problem solving involving technology, building on work already started in some of the schools under the aegis of the BP/CRAC Science and Technology initiative'. The science group made the first visible impact on the way children learn when its resource-based learning modules were introduced in spring 1988. Teachers from Fearnhill, Norton, St Francis and Willian continued to meet through 1988 and each received a weekly half-day release through the community links programme. Industrial visits were planned and, under an alternative energy banner, visits were organized to an energy-efficient Letchworth showhouse and to the local sewage works.

The energy work began with looking at contemporary power supply systems and compared them with other forms of energy production like solar, geothermal, tidal and wind energy. The students wrote word-processed letters to various companies and in one school an information pack was prepared 'to see ways in which they could present the module to different teaching groups'.

An Education 2000 home economics scheme was introduced in every school, though all the girls in St Francis had dropped out by 1988. During planning meetings in 1986 and 1987 the groups established their aims and objectives for years one to three. A first-year workbook was prepared and software tested out. The Multiplan financial modelling package was used to illustrate costings and the Diet program to look at energy, food and fitness. The Paint package was used to assist in textile

81

design graphics work and the Food program was introduced to some fourth-year pupils. In November 1987 a whole-day home economics workshop, pulling in special needs and adviser support, decided to redesign the worksheets. Links with the TVEI food industries course were formalized and liaison with primary schools established.

With modern languages all six schools remained under the Education 2000 co-ordinating umbrella. Tray, a software package which allows teachers to set up blocks of text with missing words that need to be correctly filled, was used widely and word processing in French and German experimented with. Initially the language teachers attended workshops exploring satellite TV (more of which in Chapter 8), BBC Basic programming and the Teletel information service. The group visited the Brealey Languages Centre in Sleaford, Lincolnshire, where they were shown a purpose-built system of work stations tied into a computer, video monitor, tape deck and headphones with access to interactive video and audio equipment and satellite TV. 'The centre,' one teacher commented, 'was severely under-used due to lack of time for staff training.'

At Highfield School and St Francis College they concentrated on using computer programs to assist the language development of second-, third- and fourth-year pupils, an exercise which confirmed for them the dearth of computer-aided language learning software available for their Nimbus computers. In another initiative a triple tape copier and bulk eraser were paid for jointly by the North Herts Teachers' Centre in Letchworth, the Education 2000 trustees and the six schools. This allows a large number of audio language tapes to be prepared and then used for homework tasks.

A special needs group worked particularly closely with the North Herts Teachers' Centre; the major concern was to introduce post-Warnock whole-school approaches to follow up work already done at Highfield. At their opening meeting they agreed to split into two working parties. The first, comprising staff from Fearnhill, Norton and St Francis, looked into special needs-related software. They settled on the Word word-

82

processing package bundled up into the Nimbus networks but reported 'the almost total lack of suitable packages for special needs pupils'. However, the word processing alone convinced them that information technology was reaping immediate benefits and the group complained of 'the lack of imagination from mainstream teachers'. It is a familiar enough complaint from special needs but one which had the more force here for being orchestrated by several schools and thus directed at several sets of staffs. Meanwhile the second group, comprising teachers from Norton, Highfield and Willian, produced an Inset package for support teaching. It examined off-the-shelf video packages and decided to buy in where necessary. There was also a call for laptop computers, which has remained unanswered for lack of funds though, at the time of writing, some of the maintained schools are still hoping to obtain some laptops as part of their TVEI work.

Religious education is a topic with the capacity to generate almost as much hot air as curriculum development itself. By the project's second stage Education 2000, along with local churches had already produced a document with the old formula that religious education by itself could not be construed as moral education because moral behaviour is not necessarily dependent on religious belief. 'We believe,' they said, 'that it is not the school's responsibility to undertake specific faith and nurture education [although] there is a Christian viewpoint to every aspect of the curriculum.'[8] A broad, if predictably bland, element of religious education had been included in the Education 2000 agenda and in Letchworth carried all the more weight for coming with a community endorsement. The often lonely and marginalized religious education teachers from four of the schools met entirely voluntarily after hours and backed sentiment with action. In April 1988 100 fifth-formers took part in a video-recorded RE Day at St Francis college. Those also present included speakers drawn from the major faiths, community support organizations and the police. A system of teacher exchange between schools was also established whereby staff shared their knowledge of particular faiths with other sets of pupils. Technology wasn't ignored and a multi-faith theme relied on 'strong information technology support for resource based learning involving video and video camera work, computerized databases and support through slide viewers and audio tapes'.

Musical education too laid claim to computers on offer through Education 2000. With the exception of Norton, all the schools formed a group which eventually chose the Atari ST20 synthesizer and, from January 1989, had a weekly meeting with the suppliers to gain expertise. This equipment has been particularly popular on GCSE course work. As one of the music teachers said:

> Its impact has been considerable, enabling us to demonstrate easily techniques which hitherto were time-consuming and often difficult to comprehend. What has become apparent to us after forming the group is that single machines will not suffice, especially with music being a compulsory in the national curriculum for older students.

Another group was formed between all the schools, well into the project's second stage, to lobby for video equipment. A host of reasons – including the recording of school plays and outings; the recording of mock interviews given to school-leavers; use in personal and social education lessons; and general cross-curricular work – made the case for buying filming kit. 'The scheme has vast potential possibly on a par with information technology', noted the trustees and then drew breath at high capital costs of £1,500 per school for camera, video, monitor and tripods. But they paid up, and five schools got equipment based around Panasonic M7 Camcorders.

One of the bolder conclusions of the curricular aspects of the Education 2000 experiment is the consideration that teaching, or learning rather, should begin to move off timetable. Indeed this approach has antecedents before Letchworth: research carried out ten years ago by the NFER is worth quoting. It showed that while schools are staffed on the assumption that four-fifths of a teacher's time is in formal classroom teaching, the reality is that only a fifth of their professional activity is in the classroom. That is something which recent legislation has not accounted for but even within classrooms there is great scope for other ways of organizing the school day. Before he moved on to become the project's associate director, Richard Dix-Pincott was leader of the Education 2000 curriculum group. He negotiated the complexities of co-ordinating timetables across six schools, which led him to some interesting ideas on how school days are organized. The following is a paraphrase of a paper he wrote on the subject.[9]

He begins by asserting that schools have traditionally been organized for the benefit of teaching rather than learning. Why else, he asks, would secondary schools require their pupils to put down what they are doing before they are finished to move on to another place and another activity? He says that schools must radically reorganize their use of time to allow for the extended periods of study which are already a feature in most primary schools. In recent years the drive has been to reduce the average class size (something, incidentally, which has never been on the Education 2000 agenda) to increase the contact between student and teacher. The cost of this has been a major reduction in the provision of learning resources, which has resulted in teachers having to teach in an increasingly didactic fashion. Mr Dix-Pincott points to the irony that 'a reduction of resources' has meant teachers have had less rather than more time to spend on guiding their students. 'Perhaps the one positive outcome of the present national shortage of specialist teachers,' he says, 'will be the need to provide students with learning resources from which they can work directly and not be so dependent on the teacher.' An example of this is the mathematics teacher who, on taking up his post as head of department in a large comprehensive school, discovered he was the only mathematics specialist on the staff. Other teachers who did not have a full timetable within their own subjects were required to take maths lessons. So the new teacher devised the well-known Smile individualized learning program to provide pupils with most of the resources needed so that any competent teacher, irrespective of mathematical ability, could oversee maths lessons.

Mr Dix-Pincott cites evidence that 'in this increasingly information rich society' less than half of what is learnt 'can be accounted for from within the school'. He says that schools must respond by altering their function from being deliverers of information and teaching to being brokers or agents for learning. He returns to the community element of the Education 2000 formula to stress that learning must be seen as something which takes place anywhere in the community and with schools 'coordinating resources in order to give their students access to them whether they be human or material'. In freeing teachers from the task of providing teaching materials it will be possible to concentrate more on professional development. 'School timetables,' Mr Dix-Pincott concludes, 'must be reconstructed to become aids to life in the school and not, as they persistently are in most schools, a constraining force.'

On the principle that constant change from lesson to lesson is an inhibition to learning, several Letchworth schools have gone off timetable to allocate longer periods of time to complex tasks. In the lower school at St Christopher days have been set aside to produce a newspaper using *The Times* newspaper's online information service plus local newspaper and radio newsrooms. On another day St Christopher pupils used a computer link-up to French schools and the French viewdata service to plan a day trip across the Channel. Another set of pupils went through the process of manufacturing a new brand of sweets and devised packaging and marketing ideas. It brought together four departments – home economics, art, CDT and business studies – as well as demanding levels of teamwork not common in most secondary schools. The Fearnhill sixth-formers had two similar days off normal timetable. The first was spent working with the Find Your Feet Third World charity on projects for putting useful technologies into remote areas. The second involved taking an eighteenth-century house which had fallen into disrepair, preparing a restoration programme and then suggesting ways of furnishing it in the style of the time.

According to Richard Dix-Pincott,

> All these projects gave students the opportunity to acquire skills which would be of fundamental importance to them and yet do not feature in any great detail within the national curriculum. They gave them a realization of how many things have to be linked together to achieve success and what can happen if one link fails. They gave the teachers an insight into how they might pool their time to create far more interesting learning experiences for their students which would enable true learning skills to be acquired as well as the more traditional content so beloved of examination syllabuses and secretaries of state.[9]

The shift from teaching to learning has embraced a multitude of other changes. It was almost inevitable that a town's reorganization of its schools brought with it some challenges to the local education authority structure. From curriculum reappraisal came ideas of new timetables with challenges to the new status quo, and this can be reported on as a challenge to some of the values which inform the national curriculum. But there has been a consensual twist to the timetable reappraisal and the place this has most clearly been demonstrated are the school libraries where, for example, most of the special projects were centred. The libraries were included in Education 2000 plans for curriculum development because they are naturally both cross-curricular (in that most of a school's reference books on every subject are there) and they operate beyond the timetable that goes on in other school rooms. But, when they are not silent and unused, most school libraries are merely places to shelter from bad weather, whereas in Letchworth they have become the busy hub of the school academic life.

Notes

1 Sayer, John (1985) *What Future for Secondary Schools?* Brighton: Falmer Press.
2 *Better Schools* (1985) DES White Paper. London: HMSO.

3 *Red Book Three, Curricula 11–16: Towards a Statement of Entitlement* (1983). London: Her Majesty's Inspectorate.
4 DES (1982) *Planning the Curriculum as a Whole.* London: HMSO.
5 *Curriculum Policy for Schools* (1984) Hertfordshire County Council.
6 Abbott, John (1984) *Towards a Secondary Curriculum Appropriate for the Year 2000: A Summary of Main Points in the Feasibility Study known as 'Hertfordshire 2000'.*
7 *Annual Report* (1988) Education 2000.
8 *Annual Report* (1987) Education 2000.
9 Dix-Pincott, Richard *Report of the Education 2000 Curriculum Group.* Education 2000.

8 The libraries

While he was in Letchworth Kenneth Baker was photographed sitting at a table in the Fearnhill school library and chatting to nervous-looking schoolboys. Standing behind him, their faces wreathed in concern, are the project director Tom Corkill, the then headmaster of Fearnhill, Richard Dix-Pincott, and the Education 2000 director, John Abbott. They needn't have looked so worried for Mr Baker drew exactly the conclusions they wanted him to:

> I went into the library of one of the Letchworth schools. When you go into a school library it is usually one of the quietest and emptiest parts of the school, where the books nestle on the shelves barely taken out. And what was so interesting about this particular library, there were computers all around and teams of people working with computers and also working on projects on the books behind. And they had got to the stage of the facility you would like to see; there was real [keyboard] facility.

What Mr Baker saw wasn't merely a stage-managed set-up. On many visits to the schools, where I have arrived without pomp or warning, I have found the same activity in the libraries. Much of the attraction is that each library is home to many computers. When the bell rings for break times one lot of pupils is levered away from the screens because, whatever the weather, more children are waiting their turn. Give them a chance and they'll describe a Byzantine system of passes designed to regulate the flow of keenness. At most schools the children carry round their own 3.5 inch discs which are shovelled into the computers with expert fingers. The policy of open access has brought its problems and at one school, amidst rumours of computer viruses and teenage sabotage, their systems kept on crashing for no reason anybody could discover. It took all Nick Peace's expertise as information technology manager to diagnose that one boy's disc was smeared in marmalade and that this breakfast transfer was thwarting technology transfer.

Some children rush to the computers to write essays, others get on with compiling a newsletter or magazine, while others play games. One Monday afternoon, after the Norton school day was officially over, Scott McGuire took his place at one of the Nimbus terminals. 'In the juniors,' he says, 'there was nothing to do after school. Now I'm usually here on Mondays, Wednesdays and Thursdays.' He is a first-year and says the word processing he's been learning is easy. What he wanted to show off was his skill on PC Paint, a graphics package he said he had been taught to use by one of his friends. Mouse to hand, he drew an elaborate spacecraft and filled out a black background dotted with stars. He called up another program from the school network's database and I left him playing a computerized version of snooker that demanded correct calculation of the angles the cue ball was likely to take. That he'd learnt to do all this without help from a teacher is another key feature of Education 2000. For another example of what one teacher called 'a high level of unforced peer teaching', the sixth-formers who worked on the house restoration project mentioned at the end of the last chapter used unfamiliar software packages and each team was joined in the library by a third-year pupil attached as an information technology consultant.

'No longer are libraries seen solely as the repositories of the written word', says a submission, written by Tom Corkill, to the Jerwood Award which is given to those deemed to have made original and significant contributions to the theory and practice of education.

The libraries are truly becoming the resource centres of the schools and important results are evident from work being done. The first is the way in which many departments who have never been traditional users of the library now see it as a valuable support to their lessons and actively work with the library teams to improve the resources for students. Commonly teachers from these departments now use the library as a starting point for many of their lessons. The second is the increased use of written materials in the library and more books are now being borrowed or referred to. Far from reducing the use of books the information technology has made them more accessible for many students.[1]

Christine Dodds, the librarian at Fearnhill School, confirmed that one of the effects of computers was that 'use of the library has snowballed out of all proportion to how it was before'. In between telling some fifth-formers how to use key words in their search for books on a physics problem, she explained how Education 2000 money had been spent on a lot else besides computers. There is a clerical assistant who spent a year cataloguing the 10,000 books in the library. There is a good deal of new shelving and a couple of video monitors. Talk came back to the technology and she showed a compact disc machine. Its most entertaining package is Domesday, a monster survey of British life in the early 1980s complete with 23,000 colour-screen shots of British towns, 24,000 Ordnance Survey maps and a huge socioeconomic database. Hours of fun. Then there is the ECCTIS compact disc database, which sixth-formers use to find out about their higher education opportunities. The Educational Counselling and Credit Transfer System lists over 50,000 higher education courses and, particularly in the final term, is the disc which means the compact disc terminal gets a regular hammering. But even before Christmas a couple of sixth-formers were searching for a future. It looked straightforward enough to use.

One thought she might like to study travel or hotel management but these didn't work as key words. 'Try tourism,' said the other. She pushed the F2 key again and typed tourism when the screen prompt demanded 'subject'. Up peeled the information that there are 335 higher education courses under tourism, so they asked what was available locally. They scrolled through a narrowed list of 35 options. First was a course demanding a degree and published work. 'I don't think a year's part-time waitressing at a Little Chef would count, do you?' Half an hour later – time which was used for talking rather than keyboard jabbing – and they left the library with a printed list of ten or so likely courses.

'What is clear to the schools,' Tom Corkill wrote in his competition entry, 'is that young people need and deserve the very best information possible delivered to their place of work. What we cannot ignore is the steadily growing demand from students and teachers alike to have first class information available at an economic price.' And that is the major drawback, for this stuff isn't cheap. Hardware starts at £1,500 and a complete Domesday package costs £4,500. Christine Dodds, however, doesn't simply talk about money for technology. She showed where a door was going to be knocked through from the sixth-form study area of the library to a computer room next door which she felt would establish even closer links between old-fashioned books and the new databases. She talked of the greater liaison she now had with departments who had each appointed a member of staff to let her know what books to order, and who had an 8 per cent increase on their book-buying budgets. She talked of the Education 2000-funded release periods during which she met librarians in the other schools for the first time and the many visitors she'd shown round the library. All this was what was originally intended: the Education 2000 library initiative was one of the areas, along with craft design technology, science, home economics and modern languages, which had been identified as part of school life where cross-curriculum development could most readily be stimulated. Libraries, after all, are easily recast as 'information databases' and are the only academic parts of schools which are not pinned to any particular area of the curriculum.

Initially two schools, Fearnhill and St Christopher, were the only ones involved, with briefs to 'pilot schemes capable of dissemination in the long term'. Librarians from the other four schools soon demanded a slice of the action and they equalled craft design technology and religious education teachers in their enthusiasm to meet colleagues from other schools. Therefore project support during 1987 and 1988 included staff enhancement of 0.6 to Fearnhill and 0.4 to St Christopher with a brief 'to facilitate the development of the library as a multi media resource base, liaison with departmental staff and dissemination across the town'. Other schools got smaller chunks of staff enhancement time, again calculated to a formula which reflected the number of pupils they have.

Each school library was given six Nimbus microcomputers and put in bids to the Education 2000 trust to acquire its own mix of microfiche readers, video recorders and compact disc machines; this soon had the effect of broadening out the curriculum. The Farmlink portion of Prestel, for example, was subscribed to for pupils from geography, environmental studies and business studies to discover the information that forms part of a farmer's stock in trade. Those teachers assigned to library liaison, first from special needs, design and mathematics and later from social studies, languages and creative arts, got Inset time in the library. A 'dissemination meeting' was held in November 1987 and to help pupils find their way through all the newness a number of booklets were written and distributed through the six schools: *Help With Study Skills*; *Learning and Revision*; *Writing Essays*; *Learning How to Learn*; *Sixth Form Study Guide to the Library*; *Audio Visual Indexes*; and guides to ECCTIS and Prestel.

Meanwhile at the two 'library project schools' Nigel Coulthard, the head of English at Fearnhill, and Simon Armitage, the librarian at St Christopher, had set about discovering the database package to catalogue their library stocks. But not before they'd produced a broader specification detailing what their libraries should be achieving. Simon Armitage's contribution to the St Christopher project specification, a document all schools had to submit to the Education 2000 trustees, deserves quoting in full as it gives a model for how to technologize a library. Mr Armitage starts by noting co-operation with Fearnhill – the kind of co-operation between a state and a private school which, like most other Letchworth teaching staff, he barely bothers to comment on any more. He continues:

PROGRESS 1987/88

1. Review of existing stock in the library, including integration of departmental material on to main catalogue.
2. Installation and evaluation of a variety of information and systems (Prestel, *The Times* Newspaper Service, Ceefax, Teletel, video and satellite reception and recordings).
3. A search for a suitable computer based catalogue and information retrieval system for resources sited throughout the school, including Keywording Thesauri.

AIMS: GENERAL

1. To continue review and update of library stock in consultation with teaching staff.
2. To develop a central resource area in the library with facilities for access to a range of media and information sources.
3. To evaluate stock held in departments and to integrate into central resources/catalogues as appropriate.
4. To evaluate and introduce a computerized library management system.

AIMS: STAFF

1. Establish a library development group with a cross-curricular group of staff.
2. Representatives of departments to undertake stock review with library staff.
3. Development of resource materials for specific curriculum areas in humanities and modern languages.
4. All new staff to have library induction sessions.

AIMS: PUPILS

1. To have an introduction to information retrieval systems.
2. To have open access, including evenings and weekends [i.e. for St Christopher's boarders] to a range of media – video with foreign language satellite recording, tape/slide and teletext.
3. To undertake project work that requires the planned use of library resources.

4. All pupils to have library induction sessions, at an appropriate level on arrival and subsequently on an annual basis.

STAFFING NEEDED

1. Enhanced staffing to be used to allow some release throughout the year for librarian and teachers undertaking review of stock.
2. Release for other staff using supply to enable participation in the project.
3. Allocation needed for additional professional support time, most crucially during the period of establishing a computerized management system.

RESOURCES NEEDED

1. Hardware to develop the range of resources in video and tape/slide presentations.
2. Network software for library management system.
3. Storage facilities are needed for non-book resources.

If your taste runs to ranks of hardware, the St Christopher library is the most impressive amongst the Letchworth schools. Simon Armitage's office is a glass-sided cubicle at the entrance and there is too much high technology for the eye to settle on any one item. I was attracted to the satellite-linked television bubbling with a middle-of-the-day Italian soap opera but the library cataloguing system was at the front of Mr Armitage's mind. Together he and Nigel Coulthard, his opposite number at Fearnhill School, did the rounds of software houses searching for a database suitable for listing their library's contents. They visited the county library and the most ambitious thing considered was the Calm library management minicomputer system from Pyramid, though this was eventually ruled out as too expensive. It is a measure of the scope given to each school that they eventually put in successful bids for differing solutions both, though, reliant on Research Machines microcomputers.

Down the road at Fearnhill Mr Coulthard selected a software package from the Schools Integrated Management System range. (SIMS is produced by a spin-off from the Bedfordshire local education authority and the whole suite of programs is one of the most popular for schools automating for local financial management.) By April 1989 some 10,000 books had been listed, mostly by a clerk whose salary was paid by Education 2000, and Mr Coulthard had written the Fearnhill School Library Management Guide. The days I visited the Fearnhill library, the SIMS database was certainly getting regular use. Mr Armitage said:

> In a lot of respects SIMS is excellent and, at £250, very cheap. However I didn't think it good enough as it is designed for books only and I wanted to input video and slide references as well. Its problem was inflexibility as the database fields are already so tightly defined it did not leave me enough room to specify what I wanted.

Instead he plumped for the free text Elrond database from Head Computers and put up a sufficiently good case for the Education 2000 trust to stump up the £1,500 it cost. Over the 1989 summer holidays Mr Armitage and a sixth-former, with some help from Head Computers which wants to sell its system to other schools, typed in the 16,000 items to another computerized library catalogue which is now also up and running.

Mr Armitage did a quick review of the other kit in his library and pointed to the back of pupils' heads: 'Those ones over there are on the Nimbus network, though I really couldn't tell you what they are doing. I think that girl over there is into the Telecom Gold electronic mail system.' Another boy, too busy to pay much attention to my questions, had logged into the Ebenezer conferencing terminals. Mr Armitage told how the online links with schools in France and Germany had been used to set up a German exchange in Fulda and a French exchange at Commercy near Nancy. Despite all this Mr Armitage is not a routine Education 2000 convert. 'The library is definitely busier since the project started,' he said, 'though sometimes I think that has more to do with students preparing GCSE course work. You might even say that GCSE has acted as a stimulus on Education 2000.' So, with the exception of the hardware, Mr Armitage's verdict of Education 2000 is that

'it hasn't made a huge difference'. At Fearnhill Mr Coulthard
disagreed:

> Although I was sceptical at first and thought big business money
> would dominate to try and persuade us to produce fodder for the
> factories, it has not turned out that way. In fact business hasn't
> wanted to dictate educational terms at all. To my mind, though
> the computers are very important, they are secondary to work
> we've been able to do on the curriculum. Education 2000 has
> given teachers more time to think and what we have established
> here has been, unlike a bolt-on initiative such as TVEI, built into
> the system.

Funds or no funds for the 1989 school year, the Fearnhill
library has been reorganized in a way that has drawn in the
academic departments and Mr Coulthard, his early scepticism
about taking industry handouts defused, seems pleased enough
with that.

Back at St Christopher it was hard to imagine anything so
base as mere scepticism from the German teacher, Edwin
Gruber. He's found salvation through technology and since
the project started has spent increasing amounts of time in the
library. 'Watch the European broadcasts', he tells his sixth-
form language students. 'You can see in their results who has
been watching the satellite TV,' he told me. 'How many teachers do you know who tell their pupils to watch more television?' Pinned to the librarian's door is a rota detailing what
evenings the satellite receiver has been fixed on to French,
German, Italian or Spanish broadcasts. He says the rota is
necessary, since the tuning equipment has to be stored behind
locked doors for it is too sensitive for the pupils to handle.
Mr Gruber told of a lesson he'd done that afternoon with a
videotape from the satellite receiving equipment in the library.
They'd watched a news feature item about a macho Frenchman
who skied down hills at 100 m.p.h. 'Listening to him talk was
something funny and we saw action while we learnt grammar
and vocabulary.'

Fearnhill, which has the Letchworth schools' other satellite dish, and St Christopher regularly record news bulletins and send out video cassettes to the other schools. But it takes time to do the editing and Mr Gruber pines for go-faster dubbing and tape splicing kit. But he's content with the fast tape copier now installed across town at the North Herts Teachers' Centre and tickled by the funding arrangement that each school pays £60 towards its cost. As for the satellite equipment itself, he's convinced it is worth the money: '£1,500 for everything including the dish,' he says. 'It is used constantly and easily covers itself.' The use of the foreign broadcasts extends beyond exercises in foreign languages. During the European Community Madrid summit, for example, many pupils saw news and comment programmes from Spain, Germany and France and were able to discuss how events were interpreted outside the UK.

Mr Gruber has taught at St Christopher for seven years but, prior to Education 2000, had not met language teachers from elsewhere in the town. The language teachers' curriculum group still meets occasionally, he says, in spite of the money for their release time drying up. 'Of course I can't put a price on the good will that has been built up,' says Mr Gruber. 'But I have found it invaluable.' He also leads the inter-schools video group and talks of 'lobbying and pleading for eighteen months' to get video cameras. In the end Education 2000 paid half the cost of the cameras and tripods that were bought for a multi-curricular bunch of lobbyists including teachers of language, English, drama and science.

We met one evening at St Christopher, where Mr Gruber lives with his family, and he was anxious to get back to making a half-hour tape from four hours of West German coverage of migrations from the East. He had a lot else on his mind too. Having contrasted British education to the one he was brought up in in Austria ('too much specialization here too early . . . but . . . more individualism'), he talked of mixing age levels as well as abandoning streaming. Mr Gruber, who gets many of his brighter students through their GCSE at the end of their fourth year, was buzzing and he reminded me of what John Abbott had said on my first trip to Letchworth. In his estimation: 'Most teachers are idealistic and we want to empower them to grasp back that idealism.'

Notes

1 Corkill, Tom (1989) *The Jerwood Award*. Award submission made by Education 2000.

9 Pupils and teachers
'The needs of young people as the end'

Break time at Highfield School and, as usual, Chris Hutchinson is by himself smoking his pipe at his place next to the window. He keeps himself a little apart from the rest of the Highfield staff and, being just a few years from retirement, his initial reaction to Education 2000 was stand-offish. He'd heard about too many educational initiatives in over 30 years of teaching to be enthused by Education 2000 rhetoric; its practice, however, has made him something of a convert.

It is worth recounting Mr Hutchinson's change of heart as an example of how the fourth and final component of the Education 2000 formula – 'satisfying the needs of young people' – has come to life. In 1981, some while after the publication of Baroness Warnock's report, *Education of Handicapped Children and Young People*,[1] Mr Hutchinson transferred from being head of Highfield's English department to head its new special needs department. Early on he discovered that 20 per cent of children needed the remedial attention his department was offering, which presented him with the chore of finding out who they were and then monitoring their progress. 'The essence of my job is collecting information,' he says. 'You can't make a diagnosis unless you have that information.' It was the cue for him to describe the database he's written; he showed me a sheet of computer printout listing details of children and their special needs. Further columns across a wide spreadsheet contained notes like 'can't link ideas ... verbal diff ... gives up easily' and the final columns outlined the teaching programmes of each special needs pupil. 'By having all the information stored reliably in

100

a single place,' says Mr Hutchinson, 'we get to children quicker and can be more consistent in helping them.' That success is due to Education 2000 which first had him taking a computer home and later supplied him with the machine to run the database.

Other things have earned Education 2000 his support:

> The computers we have can help remove the stigma of special needs children and are particularly useful with problems of illiteracy. Beyond this Education 2000 has brought about changes of attitudes and brought both departments and schools closer together. We've got more individual activities going on in the classrooms.

Highfield integrated its special needs teaching within mixed ability groups so he was working across the curriculum before Education 2000 had ever been heard of. But he is certain that Education 2000 has enhanced this and other cross-curricular work at Highfield. 'Nobody here is fighting Education 2000 any more,' says Mr Hutchinson. 'It has enabled us to do what we wanted to do anyway.'

Thus Mr Hutchinson's database of special needs pupils can be defined as meeting the needs of young people and therefore as exemplifying the fourth aim of Education 2000. To recap, Education 2000 began with the intention to use community as the stimulus and computers as the means to result in a better curriculum and, in a final phrase, to 'satisfy the needs of young people as the end'. Educational semantics is an endless game but an interesting one, and it betrays our uncertainties of what education is all about. The words I find irritating are the Sunday-schoolish 'young people' instead of the more common children, pupils or, at around the time of GCSEs, students. Many teachers were also unhappy with this last part of the formula, seeing it as superfluous, and as an insult in its laboured description of what they were doing already. Mary Marsh, deputy head of St Christopher, was one teacher who argued against the phrase's inclusion as part of the Letchworth pilot's summary. 'As a project component, it was stating the

101

obvious,' she says. 'And I was unclear about what the component was going to achieve on its own.'

Objection overruled, because the founders felt some kind of a formal statement was necessary to stress who the project, ultimately, was intended for. 'The needs of young people' gained currency and got its first airing in the glossy fund-raising brochure produced with the help of the Kleinwort Benson merchant bank. 'Do you know these young people? Would you welcome them into your company?' the brochure asked. What followed was a list about 'young people who are able to manage their own learning . . . who are trained to think things out for themselves . . . who, while being respectful of authority, do not wait to be told what to do . . . who live with the implications of making decisions . . . who are good communicators' and so on in a swirl of elocution which is about as helpful as an affirmation of motherhood. Elsewhere in the Education 2000 literature this bland idealism is under-pinned by the more sound perception that 'most educational thought has been adult directed with virtually no tradition of trying to understand problems of learning and decision making as experienced by young people themselves'. What evolved was a Needs Of Young People Programme whereby each of the schools appointed a co-ordinator who had half a day's release time a week to administer four projects.

First were extensions of the Personal and Social Education (PSE) courses already being given and from where the co-ordinators for this part of Education 2000 were drawn. Examples of PSE include study skills, self-evaluation, how to organize oneself, careers and health education. Second, and this fed straight back into the community component of Education 2000, there was 'liaison with external support agencies'. For example, some older pupils met local Rotarians and invited them back to their respective schools. Recalling this, Richard Dix-Pincott says:

One of the needs expressed by the students in their study groups was for the opportunity to meet and talk with normal adults. By normal they meant those who are not their teachers or close relatives. Interestingly the Rotarians, in discussing this, realized that as adults they equally very rarely spoke with young people who were not in their family. This is leading to a whole variety of different contacts between both parties.

The third part of the Needs of Young People Programme was the Young People's Study Groups. A pair of groups each with up to fourteen members, included fourth- and fifth-years and was dominated by sixth-formers. They met in various schools in a kind of debating society which drew several conclusions that were later included in the 1988 Education 2000 annual report. In what must surely be a grown-up's paraphrase of what was actually said, they were worried that 'education in schools seems to be designed to separate young people within a total community such as Letchworth and so inhibits the growth of any sense of responsibility'.[2] And there are three more equally airy points, complete with calls for 'better communications' and 'meaningful processes'. Mr Dix-Pincott makes a less harsh appraisal. 'The purpose of the groups was to provide a forum for young people to express their views on a wide range of issues, but principally on the education they were experiencing,' he says. 'I know, for example, that they produced an excellent critique of didactic teaching and what it felt like to experience it.'

The fourth and final part of this programme is a slice of pure corporate gung-ho. The Grubb Institute devised an Action Research Project 'to encourage students to test and develop their capacities to handle situations by reacting to practical questions about their life in school and society'. Its 'learning tool' was developed for the Youth Training Scheme and works on the assumption that adolescents generally underestimate their capacities during the transition from childhood to adulthood. Life Manager 2000 had fourth-, fifth- and sixth-formers examining things that might happen to them, deciding what they might do and going through a series of cards speculating on likely outcomes of their decisions. The questionnaires attached were unpopular, if only because Department of Education researchers were also burdening pupils and teachers with questionnaires.

There is a telling phrase thought important enough to appear in bold type in the entry to the Jerwood Award: 'The project asserts that the future success of young people will depend as much on their social skills as it will on their intellectual skills.' That is a more rigorous form of words than 'needs of young people', which also gets away from impaling Education 2000's success on a totting up of exam results. Although it is too early to do this, because the first group of the first-years the project has concentrated on won't be sitting their GCSEs until 1992, there is a reluctance in Letchworth to have the pilot assessed simply according to exam results. Laurie Robinson, who did a year's secondment as project director of the new Ipswich Initiative, Suffolk 2000, is more explicit. 'If we don't get better overall GCSE results in five or six years' time,' he says, 'I will wonder why we have been doing it. However, I expect that the initiative in Ipswich will benefit the average and the below average the most.'

Therefore the most that can usefully be said about public examination results (which many of the founders of Education 2000 suspect is the very mechanism to have written off the majority of people's school careers as a failure) is that they may or may not be a yardstick by which to assess what has gone on in Letchworth. So how else are we to tell if the experiment has worked? Have the enthusiasm, the teacher training, the computers and the co-operation between schools been worth that investment of just over £100 per pupil? What results has the 'laboratory-type programme' promised in the Kleinwort Benson brochure yielded?

On my first visit to Letchworth I was shut in a room with a group of 12-year-old Highfield pupils. That in itself was a mark of the school's confidence because schools, like any other institution, usually favour a journalist with a minder who sticks close by until the journalist and notebook are politely ushered off the premises. The Highfield children were full of confidence and eager to answer my questions. They did so all at once so I didn't hear much, though a general complaint was that there wasn't enough time at the computers to do all they wanted. When I enquired whether they liked their school or not, it was as if David Frost had asked a TV studio full of middle-aged Iowans if they supported the American flag. From a babble of enthusiasm I picked the voice of Amanda Walker who said: 'They treat you like human beings here. It's not the same as junior school where they didn't take any notice of you unless you were naughty.' Though this doesn't qualify as rigorous research, when I popped the same question on later visits to children at other schools I invariably got the same kind of happy response. Had any adult been allowed into Bushey Grammar School to ask if I was enjoying myself there, I'd have thought they were mad. Of course I was never asked.

Perhaps the Letchworth pupils are more used to visitors than most schoolchildren but there is little of the perplexed surliness that teenagers often show under scrutiny. But getting them to say anything intelligible about Education 2000 is difficult as they have nothing to compare it with. They'll say 'it is education in a different way using computers' or 'mixing up subjects like at junior school' or 'more variety' or 'helping us get a job'. It is better to get them talking of specifics; of how Fiona Soloman, a boarder at St Christopher, writes a semi-punctuation-free letter home before tracing the cursor back over her word-processed script to insert commas and apostrophes; of how Richard Clowser, a third-year at Norton school, seems to know all about his computer's insides and prefers working alone, while next to him Heidi Woodworth and Catherine Hunt are indifferent to all that but like working together on their essays; of how another Norton boy, a shy first-year called Scott McGuire, has discovered a nifty way to thwart the scoring routine on a simulated darts game which makes it impossible to beat him; or of how Tom Szirtes, a fifth-year at St Christopher, has laid out the Community Services Volunteers' newsletter; or how Katherine Todd, a second-year at Highfield, is writing a detective story; or how her friend built the sturdiest of pedestals, which easily took her weight

105

but was criticized by her craft design technology teacher as 'over-engineered'.

What excited Lord Limerick, who toured Letchworth when he was deputy chairman of Kleinwort Benson, was the sense of concentration and relaxed self-discipline; he recalled that

> Ten strangers entered the room but no head was raised. My own memory of a classroom is that all work stopped when a single stranger entered. Groups of two or three children, absorbed in manipulating their work on screen just went right on with it. They were engrossed in what they were doing. The teacher moved round like a big brother, available to help with fresh problems.

He too, like many visitors before and since, obviously approved of what he found. Like nearly everyone who is called on to make an educational judgement, Lord Limerick relied on his own dimly recollected experience of school and, as I noted in Chapter 7, these memories are what can make every Tom, Dick or Harry (or Noble Lord or journalist) sprout instant wings of educational expertise. It's one of the things that makes a teacher's job a very hard one.

'Any judgement on education,' says John Abbott, 'is bound to be an emotional one. However, it is possible to sense when something is right or wrong and you ignore this gut reaction at your peril.' This is another way of saying that evidence of Education 2000's success is bound to be impressionistic and I can only say that the friendliness of the children, their commitment to their work, the lack of formality about the lessons and their clamouring around full libraries made a strong impression on me. Still more remarkable is the support and enthusiasm for Education 2000 from the Letchworth teachers. Letchworth is certainly not an unsullied haven of professional happiness and its teachers still feel the general malaise that afflicts nearly all teachers. Their feelings are summarized by an *Observer* leader article written in July 1989 I found pinned to the Fearnhill notice-board; the following words had been underlined.

Teachers have never been so demoralised and are drifting away from the profession. . . . Ministers pushed through a ragbag of reforms inspired more by ideology than the needs of children. . . . Teachers cannot accept the good faith of a government which has denigrated their efforts and failed to give them their reasonable reward. Meanwhile these same demoralised teachers are being called on to carry out a package of reforms intended to transform our schools. Circulars, reports, guidelines pour in daily, like the worst nightmares of a socialist bureaucracy, overwhelming heads and their staff and creating a new layer of administrative work that separates teachers form live contact with their pupils. . . . They [i.e. 'R.A. Butler's Conservative successors'] have devised a hotchpotch system which the strong can exploit while the weak go to the wall, guided by the overriding principle that as little as possible must be spent on education. Our children deserve better.

Despite these general sentiments about their position and their place, the teachers in the Letchworth secondary schools are most definitely not discontented with Education 2000 and there is any amount of favourable testimony to be had from them. I only met one who thinks the whole thing is a waste of time and such a high level of unanimity about an education initiative singles Letchworth out as something special. To make a truism out of a slogan, meeting the needs of young people requires teachers whose own needs are satisfied. The head-teachers supported Education 2000 from the beginning, if at first only because of the extra cash it promised to add to squeezed capitation budgets. They soon extended their enthusiasm and the comment of one, who was quoted in the 1988 annual report, could stand for them all: 'I can hardly believe what has happened to my staff. Education 2000 has drawn from them things which neither I, nor they, believed were possible.'

Danny Walton, the Fearnhill craft design technology teacher, pulled out a log book detailing his Education 2000 time for meetings and learning about the computers. It lists 85 hours though Mr Walton reckons he gave twice that amount. But he didn't want to be considered a fool and had this reminder: 'Don't get me wrong. Though I would say people are enjoying themselves more, we've got problems here like any other school.' There were two sets of problems he was talking about: one, the whole government stance which, at the beginning of Education 2000, led to the long teachers' dispute and which in turn delayed the start of much of the project by a year, until September 1986; two, the initial scepticism teachers had about Education 2000, a scepticism which wasn't defused until far into the project.

In February 1986, when the teaching dispute was at its height, the Letchworth joint committee of the teachers' union met for the first time at Willian school. It comprised representatives from the National Union of Teachers, the National Association of Schoolmasters and Union of Women Teachers and the Assistant Masters and Mistresses Association. That the NUT, NAS/UWT and AMMA found common ground is in itself a tribute to the magnetic effect of Education 2000, and one of their resolutions was 'to make personal contact with members of staff at St Francis and St Christopher [the two independent boarding schools] and ask them to discuss the sending of a representative of their staff to join the group'.

Nonetheless it wasn't an entirely happy group, since it complained of 'the apparent secrecy of the discussions currently taking place in the working parties'. They were bothered about conditions of service and clearly did not feel this was the 'bottom up' scheme they'd been reading about in Education 2000 papers. On 7 March John Abbott met them and explained that only the heads and deputies of the four state schools were then involved in planning and preparation and that, but for industrial action, there would have been wider staff involvement. The teacher reps stressed the importance of good communications and pointed out that industrial action was not wholly to blame for its lack. Why, the teachers asked, would the organizers of Education 2000 not go into print? The minutes of the meeting state, somewhat gnomically, that: 'These points were accepted by John Abbott who hoped that in future there would be an atmosphere of greater confidence.'

The teachers' reps also reported anxieties about conditions

of service and the two-year contracts for the extra Education 2000 staff to cover for the inter-school groups and the Inset time. Mr Abbott reassured them that the Herts County Council would continue to be the employing agency and would therefore be responsible for negotiating contracts. Underlying these concerns was the entirely separate issue of the county's secondary review and the likely closure of one of the Letchworth schools. Perhaps the only lesson to be drawn here is that every town which considers using the Education 2000 model will have something making it a special case: nothing in education is ever quite typical.

Some of the teachers' worries were never entirely dissipated. At an October 1987 meeting of the joint governors and union representatives there were complaints about Inset provision and the timetabling of community enhancement. John Abbott also used his time there to remind them that 'the project is not just about technology, it is about helping to create a rounded person'. Then in July 1988 'there was much discussion of the Education 2000 meetings outside of school hours ... [and] ... differences in interpretation which some schools were counting within the 1,265 hours of directed time'. With central government directives being so insultingly specific to people it used to deem professionals, the goodwill for which John Abbott appeals consistently is bound to be in short supply from time to time.

John Abbott's trip to America had taken him to the Schenley High School and Teaching Centre in Pittsburgh, which was established as a kind of teaching hospital to stimulate a locally devised core curriculum based on an agreed method of teaching. Some 50 extra staff were employed, largely funded by the various charitable trusts which proliferate in America, to enable Pittsburgh's 750 teachers to spend a term being retrained. John Abbott was impressed but judged it an inadequate model for its disruption of the teaching and the subsequent resistance by the staff. They didn't, he says, feel they had ownership of the scheme, unlike the other project which so influenced him in Princeton.

Earlier on, while headmaster at Alleyne's, John Abbott had tried to respond to Lord Bullock's report on the teaching of English. *A Language for Life* had stressed the importance of language development being supported across the curriculum by teachers in every subject using their disciplines to improve a general use of language.[3] It seemed a sound notion to him but his scheme for teaching communication skills met with staff resistance; they rejected something they saw as being parachuted in from the outside. 'I organized a meeting between parents and teachers and 40 per cent of my staff boycotted it,' he recalls. 'Try as I did, I could not interest them in wanting to give such explicit priority to the development of communication skills.' By 1980 he had discovered 'the new electronic technology as a powerful catalyst to transform some aspects of the learning process'. But the few computers there were at Alleyne's were the preserve of three or four fanatics in the maths department and his arguments for one computer for every child, while they attracted more of his staff this time, foundered on local authority incomprehension. 'What I learned then,' he says, 'is that you need to win the support of influential groups.' In playing such a large part in raising £1.5 million from private sponsors, John Abbott has certainly succeeded in convincing many other 'influential groups' of the sense of what he is saying. Yet his need to convince all around him has brought problems.

Since joining Education 2000 John Abbott has been making a dual appeal to the financial gentlemen as well as the teaching players and this has sometimes made it difficult to disentangle the project's educational and promotional pronouncements. A judgement, for example, on the success (or failure) of something as slippery as 'the needs of young people' would be hard, on conventional educational criteria. But when there is a parallel demand to mollify and convince past and potential donors the problem becomes even harder.

A full and dispassionate judgement on the effects of the project must await the evaluation team's report to the Department of Education in September 1990. Meanwhile other impressionistic judgements can be made, even discounting John Abbott's enthusiasm which, I must say, I have never done. However, his bold words were not what convinced me that this book was worth writing. Instead I was impressed by the unaffected enthusiasm of the pupils I met and what has turned out to be the unanimous support of the teachers, for which we can take the word of the gentle but hard-headed Chris Hutchinson at Highfield: 'Nobody here,' he told me, 'is fighting Education 2000 any more.'

Notes

1 Warnock, Mary (1978) *Education of Handicapped Children and Young People*. London: DES.
2 *Annual Report* (1988) Education 2000.
3 DES (1975) *A Language for Life: Report of the Committee of Inquiry* (Bullock Report). London: HMSO.

10 The future

The schools in Education 2000's first project have been the most frequently visited schools in Britain, with visitors once every four days or so. A Letchworth tour of inspection has been squeezed into the agenda of those listed at the beginning of this book and hundreds of others have been there too, including representatives from future Education 2000 projects and from the City Technology Colleges. In the sense of having attracted so much interest, Letchworth's schools are the most popular in the country. Not, of course, that this is a measure of success; the large crowds who watch Manchester United have not made it Britain's most successful football team. So far, if we ignore the Ipswich initiative and preliminary studies made in several northern towns, the interest of many influential people has not yet translated into as much national activity as the project leaders would have hoped for. There are many reasons for this.

Education 2000 is a complex amalgam of educational thinking which isn't readily broken down into a single phrase. 'Educating people for change' is not particularly vivid and is distracting because it's easily taken as 'educating people for a change'. The other slogan, 'From teaching to learning', takes some untangling and, according to Education 2000's own literature: 'The process is elusive to describe and difficult to do.' My swiftest explanation is of an alternative model to the City Technology Colleges which builds on existing secondary structures and gets a whole town's schools working together. It has identified generalized discontent with state education and blended money and business rhetoric from the right with liberal/leftist concerns about empowering pupils and teachers. Then it has spiced the mixture with computing. Consensus is the best word for it.

The media haven't been quite as influential in spreading this complex message as had been anticipated. It is true that there has been saturation coverage compared with most schools, including several TV news stories, a video by Nigel Hawthorne, star of the television programme *Yes, Prime Minister*, and an Open University broadcast. But the project hasn't forced its way to the centre of the educational agenda. 'In this we recognize a serious failure,' says an internal report. 'Through ignorance of the difficulties, no systematic publicity strategy has been devised.' It may not be such a failure, though, because consensus, in a decade used to confrontation as the stimulus for institutional change, doesn't yield good news angles. Those rely on a steady stream of ideological clashes which have largely been lacking from Letchworth, where an unspectacular and continuing agreement between state and private schools and less than averagely discontented teachers have been the order of the day. The local press remains convinced the whole thing is 'about computers'. The national press has paid some attention, but not one of the dailies or the teachers' trade papers has monitored Letchworth's progress as closely as the more newsworthy rival City Technology Colleges.

John Abbott talks of 'the lack of public appreciation of the importance of education'. If that is the case, it is an indifference which will apply as much to Letchworth schools as to any others. However bright the lighthouse shines, many will simply ignore it. In October 1988 Mr Abbott addressed an audience of academics at Cambridge University's Sidney Sussex College:

> We are largely unaware of the resentment of large sectors of the population who feel that they were rejected by their schools and rejected by criteria which they felt were largely inappropriate to them. This resentment is found at all levels. I was startled recently to hear a member of parliament attack the way in which academics could argue for something she felt in her bones to be wrong. Very

many people feel in their bones that their schooling did not give them what they needed; they are cross and they will no longer give education the benefit of the doubt.

Thus, according to Mr Abbott, a lack of appreciation tips into the barely concealed hostility to education which, for example, has made teacher-bashing seem a reasonable way for a politician to gather votes.

'The visits have imposed a considerable burden on the schools,' says Richard Dix-Pincott:

> They are vital to show as many people as possible at first hand what is being done and to convince them of the quality of the enterprise. Our aim is to provide not the politicians but the man in the street with the evidence of what can be possible if investment is put into education and thus generate a political pressure on the politicians. It can be likened to the health service debate where the government's stance is that costs are prime. There is developing within the country a groundswell of opinion that the health service is more important than that and has to be treated sensitively and as a national asset.

This may or may not be true but what is beyond dispute is that the Letchworth model is now being applied elsewhere. The Ipswich initiative: Suffolk 2000 is using lessons from Letchworth in its eight maintained comprehensive schools and four independent boarding schools. Ipswich too has its brochure with the Education 2000 logo and an echo of the rhetoric 'that the ability to be a life-long effective learner will be essential in our increasingly technological society'. The project started in September 1988 with the secondment of a headteacher to act as project director. Laurie Robinson, head of Thurlestone High, spent a year spreading the gospel and, Education 2000 being a complex beast, found he was having to dispel three misconceptions: first, it's only to do with computers; second, it's yet another initiative to get money out of industry; and third, it's a way of making schools produce factory fodder. Instead Mr Robinson sees it as a way of giving teachers more time, something he appreciated on his secondment, and a coherent training approach to improve on the fragmented INSET model. Most of all he sees it as a co-operative way forward, using computers as a catalyst, to 'get the advantages of City Technology Colleges without the drawbacks'.

Rather than drawing funds from Education 2000, Ipswich is operating a franchise arrangement with the trust, which has included consultancy time from John Abbott, Tom Corkill, Richard Dix-Pincott and Nick Peace. Its aims are very similar. By 1994 it hopes that a fifth of Ipswich's teachers will have done industrial placements and, for the biggest slice of their budget, all teachers will have had space in their timetable for inter-school work away from their classrooms. Curriculum managers were appointed from each subject in every school and throughout the autumn and spring terms of the 1989 school year teachers from every discipline had a series of meetings. Information technology co-ordinators were also appointed and stand-alone Research Machines Nimbus micros were made available for teachers to take home and learn; Nimbus networks will then be installed, to give one micro for every ten pupils.

Mr Robinson was succeeded as project director by another head, Stoke High's Martin Liddle. From his desk next to that of the managing director of the Willis Faber insurance company in a head office with more computers per head than a City Technology College, Mr Liddle explains Suffolk 2000's fund-raising activities which will be concentrated on the many prosperous local firms. Willis Faber was an early backer of the Letchworth project but wanted to spend its charitable money closer to home. Mr Liddle, who kept repeating the phrase 'clear community element', has to raise £2.5 million. While we talked, his phone rang: it was the Ipswich Post Office, confirming that at Christmas it will frank letters with the Suffolk 2000 emblem. 'We're also talking about their helping with the geography core curriculum by giving pupils part of a postman's training.'

Mr Liddle highlighted differences between the Letchworth

and Ipswich projects. Unlike Letchworth, Ipswich will not get money from the Education 2000 trust, which will concentrate its future energies in poor, urban districts mainly in the north of England. This second project is budgeting for the same amount of top-up funding as the first had originally intended. But the same amount will have to be spread around to cover twice as many pupils so there will not be quite as much release time for teachers and the computer-to-pupil ratio was 1:20 when they started. In this respect, times have changed since the early days of Education 2000. Unlike Letchworth, Ipswich has fuller support from its county education authority, which eventually hopes to spread the Education 2000 philosophy throughout Suffolk. The Suffolk County Council has already pitched in with £250,000 to pay, amongst other things, for the headteachers' secondments and the county information technology tutors who are doing initial computer training.

The demand for Education 2000 benefits is there from teachers and pupils. Sue Craze, who had just finished a four-afternoon course for English teachers, said: 'It was useful meeting eleven other English teachers from the Ipswich schools. No, I'd not met them before and it was interesting to find out that the private schools have less resources than we do.' Dave Munro, an information technology co-ordinator from Stoke High, said that he wanted to see computers used across the curriculum. 'We're looking to change teaching strategies. We want to build skills and adaptability for the next century, if that doesn't sound too high-falutin.' He's a pleasantly low-falutin man who suggests that, while computers are vital to the Ipswich initiative, they were merely the visible part of the project without which no industrialist could have been attracted.

Some fourth-formers who were listening in wouldn't have any of this. 'Now,' said one, 'computers are special and we want to use them every day.' Why? There was some dutiful mumbling about getting a job but what enthused them were the magazines they had produced with the school's single desktop publishing package. Ipswich initiative or not, they were already well tucked into their community and one of the magazines had £60 worth of small ads. Tim Howard, head of English at Stoke High, talked of the free sheet they are publishing with the local residents' association: 'It counts towards GCSE and gets them accustomed to deadlines,' he said. 'Most of all it means they are not writing for the teacher any more. There's a good phrase for you; I hope you use it.' I have, because it improves on promotional material droning on about moving from teaching to learning . . . children taking responsibility for their decisions . . . working co-operatively . . . developing interpersonal skills, and so on.

While the trust would be happy to support any number of franchised Education 2000 projects like Ipswich, its ambition is to set up a few, possibly only two, further fully sponsored ones. In August 1987 the trust announced its intention to help fund another project in a deprived urban locality, preferably in the north. A score or more towns put forward tentative proposals including one in West Cornwall, a Scottish town, a London borough and several southern county towns. The trust made it clear that it was a precondition of any subsequent project that the delivery of the programme would depend upon the coming together of several partners each agreeing within a contract to fund part of the project. This was the bitten biting back and in several sets of negotiations John Abbott has held out for copper-bottomed local education authority backing and more money to be committed at the outset. The drying up of the Letchworth funding is something Mr Abbott feels as keenly as any of the teachers there. Thus, according to Education 2000 policy, contracts for future funding are dependent on:

(a) the willingness of the local education authority to commit itself to providing all those elements within the programme which could, in any way, be seen as justifiable local education authority expenditure, and (b) the establishment of a local trust fund to collect donations and sponsorship for the local community. Education 2000 made it clear that, while it would do all that it could to help local communities raise their own funds, the most it itself would contribute out of national sponsorship would be no more than that raised locally. Wherever possible government grants would be sought to partner the private sector.[1]

Such stringent conditions scared off much interest and in June 1988 five towns, from the Midlands and the north, were selected for full feasibility studies. At the time of writing in November 1989, deadlines for a decision have come and gone and it is still open whether the next project will be in Bury, Calderdale, central Coventry, Leeds Chapeltown/Harehill or Wolverhampton. But Education 2000 is in no hurry and wants to do it right rather than do it fast. Where Letchworth and Ipswich are leading, others are likely to follow.

It is a mark of Education 2000's distinction and importance that its first project has been singled out for scrutiny by an evaluation team which is largely funded with £170,000 from the Department of Education. The work is similar to other evaluations of more centrally directed initiatives like TVEI, Records of Achievement and the Educational Support Grants and, to this extent, is putting Education 2000 into a national context. It is, in short, being taken very seriously indeed. The three evaluators, led by Dr Janet Ouston of the University of London's Institute of Education, have been the most regular of all the outsiders to visit Letchworth's schools.

The team reports to a DES steering group and aims to tease out the fundamentals which have been only partly addressed in the promotional literature of the trust itself. Its final report, due for publication in September 1990, should give some cool answers to the following questions: What is the project aiming to do? How has it translated this into action? What short-term effects has it had in the classroom and elsewhere? Has it increased children's self-esteem and are they more positive about self-directed learning? How effective has the new approach to in-service training been in getting away from traditional supply models? Will it stick now that the additional resources have stopped? To that end the evaluators have been

118

sitting in on lessons and, as part of a three-year study, have been sending out annual questionnaires to pupils and teachers.

Their early work cast Dr Ouston in the role of the Bad Fairy. 'Earlier this year,' said an exasperated note in Education 2000's 1988 annual report, 'there was a degree of difficulty from our point of view in comprehending the approach being used by the evaluation team as evidenced in an early interim report.'[2] What had riled them was the evaluators' initial lack of contact with the information technology co-ordinators and what they interpreted as a suggestion that the Letchworth project was being directed from the 'top down' rather than evolving 'bottom up' from the teachers. The final paragraph of the evaluation team's interim report stated:

> The Letchworth schools are not isolated from other developments in education nationally and in Hertfordshire. There are two main issues that we will be concerned with: the first is that many of the initiatives taken in the Letchworth schools are not clearly Education 2000 based. Ideas develop from the project, from local education authority and school-based Inset, from the Technical and Vocational Education Initiative and from other projects. We will not be able to disentangle the many influences on the Letchworth schools. A second factor currently of concern is the LEA secondary review. It has been proposed that one of the schools should close. It is likely that this will affect the implementation of the project.[3]

Of course the 'schools are not isolated from other developments in education'. This could never have been a test-tube experiment and it is impossible, to use the language of economists, to 'factor out' all the extraneous influences of massive external changes within education as a whole. John Abbott's metaphor here is that Education 2000 is a barrow-load of cement cohering and bonding all the other initiatives which, for the most part, are conceived in isolation from each other and often do not fit well together.

As Richard Dix-Pincott says:

> The project would be regarded as failing if it did not absorb

TVEI, the national curriculum etc. as it is all about creating the environment and climate for change. It is this eclectic approach which many find so hard to appreciate and we would regard it as a contradiction of our philosophy to attempt to factor out what was what in the schools.

Meanwhile the reservations between evaluators and project enthusiasts seem to have diminished and even that report, having grizzled about 'a degree of difficulty', concluded: 'The difficulty was overcome rapidly and the progress from that time to the present has presented no difficulty. Naturally the project is anxious to know the outcome of this evaluation.' Naturally, because Dr Ouston's analysis could make the difference between their being national pioneers or interesting local might-have-beens.

What is of interest here is the clash of visceral and cerebral approaches, a clash which raises questions about what purely quantifiable results any educational experiment can ever yield. Where John Abbott asserts that 'any judgement on education is bound to be an emotional one', Dr Ouston relies on patient statements of the research problems, a gathering of statistics over time and a refusal to leap to any conclusions or, still less, any endorsements. It is gut reaction versus a measured academic appraisal though, it must be said, it has been the gut reactions of politicians which have been the driving force behind most current educational change. And even assuming that Dr Ouston has both tangible research findings and the 'gut reaction' to lead her to unequivocal enthusiasm, the response from the politicians can only be lukewarm. Education 2000's insistence that its business sponsorship is pump-priming money to stimulate an increase in government support won't please our education ministers. They are hardly going to approve of spending even £100 per pupil a year when their autumn 1989 education spending targets allowed for 3 per cent spending rises with inflation running at over 7 per cent.

The evaluation team has picked up on Education 2000 language and has, for example, talked of studying 'the possible changes in pedagogy from teaching to learning'. More crucially, Dr Ouston has convinced the Department of Education that her team should consider the processes of change fostered by Education 2000 in Letchworth rather than, as had been the original brief, simply concentrating on its outcome. Writing in Education 2000's 1989 annual report Dr Ouston said:

> The project is a developing enterprise . . . the journey is as important as the destination . . . thus evaluation should be a continuous process rather than one that focuses on end points and outcomes only. It is, indeed, difficult to define an end point to the project since one of its aims is to set in train an approach to education that will lead to constant growth from within.[1]

And that difficulty in 'defining an end point' is another part of the assessment problem which Education 2000 itself acknowledges as the 'elusive process of describing from teaching to learning'.

What started with a conference at the beginning of the 1980s and was launched into even more turbulence than had been anticipated is now looking forward to the 1990s. It is becoming a commonplace to observe that the politics of the new decade could be more in tune with consensual approaches like that of Education 2000. If this is so, secondary education could well follow Letchworth and build on what people can agree about rather than trampling on sensibilities and forcing change through confrontation. What is certain is that yet more change is in the air. The visit to Letchworth in June 1989 by the chief executive of the City Technology College Trust, Susan Fey, brought with it suggestions of an E2K/CTC tie-in. These suggestions have been reinforced by informal links between the two charitable boards. An unpleasant pipe dream which might betray the Education 2000 consensus, or a long shot at pulling what many see as a pariah back into the mainstream educational fold?

John Abbott has learnt to be too much of a diplomat to make any intelligible comment on such speculations but he's sure, one way or another, that the broader significance of Education 2000 is still to come. In the mean time his ideas are moving fast and he's already assimilating the deeply unpopular notion of licensed teachers and seeing how it could be accepted. He deserves, in a quote which mixes a project leader's professional optimism with a teacher's professional pessimism, the last word:

> Change cannot come fast enough. Latest projections on teacher numbers would seem to suggest that, very shortly, the present structure of schooling will simply break down through lack of trained teachers. That breakdown will come at the time when technology can provide, relatively cheaply, new forms of learner interactivity, and when, within most communities, there is a growing number of qualified and recently retired professionals who could well become a new kind of tutor in a new kind of school. If all this is to be done wisely, to build on ideas which are intrinsically good and better than was done before rather than be adopted as a cost-cutting exercise or a way out of a corner, then education has to move swiftly. We need to create that powerful body of informed supportive opinion that shares a powerful vision of what we must do for the future. This is what Education 2000 is about. We feel that we have only just started.

Notes

1 *Annual Report* (1989) Education 2000.
2 *Annual Report* (1988) Education 2000.
3 DES Steering Group (1988) *Evaluation of Education 2000 . . . the Hertfordshire Project: Progress Report 2*. London: Education Management Unit, Institute of Education.

Appendix 1 National sponsors of Education 2000

Alexanders Laing & Cruikshank
Arthur Anderson and Company
Allied Lyons plc
Babcock International plc
Barclays Bank plc
The Baring Foundation
BAT Industries plc
SJ Berwin and Company
Blue Circle Industries plc
The Boots Company plc
Borg Warner Ltd
Brian Dowling Ltd
British Aerospace plc
British Airways plc
British Gas plc
BTR plc
Cadbury Schweppes Trust
Capel Cure Myers
Cazenove and Company
The Childwick Trust
The Clark Consultancy Ltd
Coats Viyella plc
Commercial Union Assurance
  Company
Consolidated Gold Field plc
Charter Consolidated plc
Country Gentlemen's Association
Courtaulds plc
Dalgety plc
Dan Air Services Ltd
The De La Rue Company plc
Department of Education and
  Science
Department of Trade and
  Industry
Digital Equipment Company Ltd

Du Pont (UK) Ltd
Eagle Star Group
The Electra Investment Trust plc
Ferranti plc
Forbes Campbell (International) Ltd
Foseco Minsep plc
General Accident plc
Harrisons and Crosfield plc
GKN plc
Glaxo Holdings plc
GT Management plc
Guardian Royal Exchange
Haden Ltd
Henderson Administration Ltd
Hogg Robinson Group plc
IBM UK Ltd
ICL
Inchcape plc
The Kleinwort Benson Group
The Sir Cyril Kleinwort
  Charitable Trust
Korn/Ferry International Ltd
John Laing plc
Lazard Brothers & Company Ltd
Letchworth Garden City
  Corporation
Lloyds: Members and Brokers
Manpower Services Commission
Midland Bank plc
Morgan Crucible Co. Ltd
Nationwide Building Society
Ocean Transport & Trading plc
Pearl Assurance plc
Pearson plc
Provident Mutual Life Assurance
  Association

The Prudential Assurance
  Company Ltd
Psion Ltd
The Rank Organisation plc
Reckitt and Colman plc
Redland plc
Reed International plc
Reed Stenhouse
Research Machines Ltd
Riverside Communications
Royal Insurance plc
Royal Ordnance plc
RTZ Ltd
Savoy Educational Trust
School Curriculum Development
  Committee
J. Henry Schroder Wagg and
  Company Ltd
The Sears Foundation
Sheppards
W H Smith Ltd
Smiths Industries plc

Spicer and Pegler Associates
St. John's College Cambridge
The Stock Exchange
The Street Trust
The Technician Education Council
TI Group plc
Touche Remnant and Company
Trinity College Cambridge
TSB Group Central Executive
The Tudor Trust
UK Atomic Energy Authority
Unigate plc
Unilever plc
Watney Mann and Truman Ltd
Williams Lea Group Limited
Willis Faber plc
Willmott Dixon plc
George Wimpey plc
Woolworths Holdings plc
Wrightson Wood Ltd

Together with generous private donations.

Appendix 2 The management structure of the project

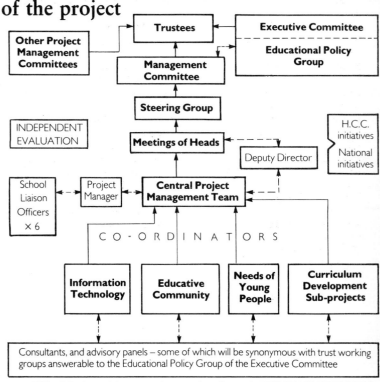

Central Project Management Team

Project manager (chairman), director/deputy director, co-ordinators, educational consultant, and other as and when required

School Management
(within each school)

```
        Head
         │
Project Manager ◄---► Education 2000 Liaison
                      and Evaluation Person ◄-----  The other agenda:
                                                    school and additional
                                                    initiatives
                                                         ▲
                                                    Deputy Director

Information Technology   Industrial   Interdependent   Needs of    Curriculum
Co-ordinator             Placements   Community        Young       sub-projects
                                                       People      where
                                                                   appropriate
```

⟶ = lines of responsibility
◄--► = flow of information

125

Appendix 3 'The three magnets'

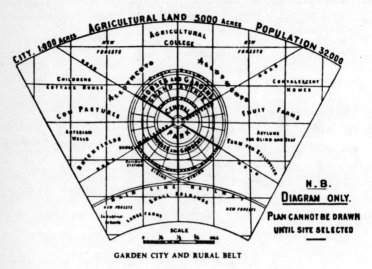

GARDEN CITY AND RURAL BELT

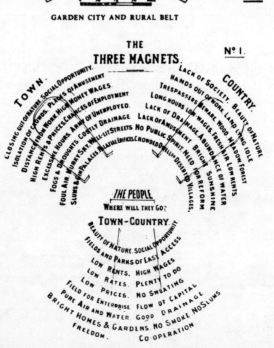

From Ebenezer Howard (1898), *Tomorrow: A Peaceful Path to Reform.*

126

Appendix 4 Information technology provision

1. Microcomputer terminals

a. **Microcomputers are RM Nimbus (PC186)**
   0.5, 1.0, or 1.5 MByte memory
   MS-DOS compatible
   colour monitor
   single or twin 3.5 inch floppy disk
   network connectable
   mouse

b. **Servers are**
   RM Nimbus AX microcomputers with 60 MBytes of winchester storage, running RM Net 2.2 software and driving RMZ Net hardware.

c. **Core software library**
   MS Word, Dataease, Multiplan, PC Paint, Contact
   MS Windows, Oriel, Excel, In-a-Vision, Aldus Pagemaker
   RM Basic, BBC Basic, RM Pascal, RM Logo

d. **Allocation of equipment**

	Computer terminals	Servers
Fearnhill	66	2
Highfield	64	2
Norton	53	2
St Christopher	29	1
St Francis	20	1
Willian	49	2

2. Ebenezer

MicroVAX II Q4 including
9 MByte memory
2 x 159 MByte disks
296 MByts Tape drive

Running Caucus communication software

There are 45 VT320 terminals distributed among the schools
and the Letchworth Garden City Corporation offices.

Appendix 5 Participants at Education 2000 national conference, May 1989

John Abbott *Organizer*	Director Education 2000 Letchworth
Jenny Bacon	Head of Schools Branch 3 DES London
Gordon Bell *Presenter*	Director Effective Learning RSA London
Derek Bowden	Head Leftwich County High School Northwich
Valerie Bragg	Principal Kingshurst CTC Solihull
David Bridges	Deputy Principal Homerton College Cambridge University
Ann Buckingham	Principal Community College Dartmouth
Gaynor Cohen	Education Adviser TVEI Basingstoke

John Cowan	Director Open University in Scotland Edinburgh
John Curtis	Head of Development TVEI London
Ray Dalton *Organizer*	Education Consultant Education 2000 Letchworth
Eric Deeson *Reporter*	Director of Resources & IT Joseph Chamberlain College Birmingham
Richard Dix-Pincott	Associate Director Education 2000 Letchworth
Peter Dutton *Organizer*	Education Adviser TVEI Sheffield
Bob Finch	Education Adviser ICI Welwyn
Heather Flint	Education Adviser TVEI London
Stanley Goodchild	Chief Education Officer Berkshire
Charles Handy *Presenter*	Chairman Royal Society of Arts London
David Hargreaves	Professor of Education Cambridge University

Peter Holly *Presenter*	Director-designate IMTEC UK Cambridge
Sue Hutchinson *Organizer*	Education 2000 Letchworth
Anne Jones *Presenter*	Director of Education Programmes Training Agency Sheffield
Martin Keating	Director Science & Learning Resources New College Swindon
Brian Knight	Honorary Research Fellow Exeter University
Bob Lewis	Co-ordinator ESRC-INTER Programme Lancaster University
Jim Lonie	Assistant Secretary Scottish Education Dept Edinburgh
Mary Marsh	Deputy Head St Christopher School Letchworth
Alan Marshall	Chief Inspector; HMI London
Nigel Paine	Assistant Director Learning Systems SCET Glasgow
Ian Pike	Head Knowle High School Blackpool

Catherine Quigley	Flexible Learning-Section TVEI London
Jean Rudduck	Head of Education Sheffield University
Dominic Savage	Director Brit. Educ. Equipment Association London
Jenny Shackleton	Principal Wirral Metropolitan College Birkenhead
Edward Simpson	Educational Consultant West Drayton
Ralph Tabberer	Schools Director NCET University of Warwick
George Tolley *Chair*	Higher Education Adviser Training Agency Sheffield
Maureen Trayers	Education Adviser TVEI London
Philip Waterhouse	National Development Centre Bristol

Those at the Consultation meeting were also most grateful for the 'Secretariat': word-processing, desk-top publishing and copying services. Learners from two Education 2000 schools in Letchworth – St Christopher School and Fearnhill – provided these.

Index